Feast
as a family

Feast as a Family: Healthy Meals That Your Family Will Actually Eat

©2018 by Allison Kloss

Published by Clovercroft Publishing, Franklin, Tennessee

Edited and Designed by Adept Content Solutions

Printed in the United States of America

ISBN: 978-1-948484-07-7

Feast
as a family

Healthy Meals Your Whole Family Will Actually Eat

Dr. Allison Kloss

With bonus recipes from Dr. Tom Stetson

Clovercroft Publishing

Acknowledgments

To my husband and daughters—thank you for your unfailing support and dedication to my passion for providing a resource for other families. Randy, the support and push you gave me to share my talent with others have been my crutch. The times when you lifted me up and encouraged me during this whole process have allowed me to achieve something bigger than myself. The father you are to our beautiful girls is something I treasure with all my heart. Thank you for being my partner in business and, more importantly, in life. My achievements are something I share with you.

To Stella, my oldest: you are amazing, and one of my favorite encouragers. Your willingness to be in photos and taste all of my food is something I hope you carry with you as you continue to make choices for your health. You are a great role model for your sister!

To Scarlett, you have brought a sense of completion to our family with your eagerness and drive. Thank you for trying all of your vegetables!

To our photographer, Brittany Wall: thank you for the amazing pictures, and for capturing the fun moments in making this book! Your talent and work ethic have been astounding and appreciated.

To Dr. Stetson: your input into this cookbook helped to make it what it is. Your friendship and ability to encourage me have been very important to this process, and I thank you for all of it.

To Drs. Zsolt and Robyn Egey-Samu: thank you for your help with the pictures and staging. I appreciate all of your encouragement throughout this process, and your excitement for this book.

To my mom, Becky: All of our time in the kitchen gave me the love for cooking. I appreciate all the patience and encouragement you have given me to not be afraid of cooking.

Contents

Prologue

by Dr. Randy Kloss

I love food, but I've never loved cooking. Experimenting, creating new recipes, and the frustration of starting over and over to make it perfect never appealed to me, which is one of the reasons I have so much respect for my wife's resilience. I've never met anyone who loves experimenting, cooking, and serving others as much as she does. I've watched her make almost every type of food I can imagine by disregarding thousands of failed attempts, keeping the ones that work, and then using her experience to benefit both our family and our patients' health.

It's never been more difficult, or more important, to make nutrition a priority in your life! I fully believe that you will find yourself coming back to this book day after day, gifting it to your loved ones, and begging for more recipes in the future.

We've used your feedback, tested the ingredients and recipes, and hope that you enjoy the result. We wish you incredible health and happy taste buds in the days to come!

Introduction

I grew up in the kitchen with my mother. I loved cooking with her and enjoyed the joy her recipes brought to our family and friends. I saw her passion for homemade dishes grow into a catering business, and she insisted every item needed to be made from scratch. I spent long nights and days helping her prepare. It was an incredible bonding experience for me, and I have since started cooking traditions with my own daughters. Great food is made in the kitchen, but more importantly, so are memories we'll have forever!

After moving away from home to attend undergraduate studies, I began to find myself eating processed foods, sugar-filled foods, and foods loaded with wheat and processed sugar. I would eat for emotional reasons and for convenience, and in the space of the next five years, I put on over sixty pounds. I would sit down to eat a piece of banana bread, only to find that I would eat the entire loaf. Pizza, pasta, and processed foods had become staples for me because they were cheap and easy to make. Food made me feel good, but I didn't understand yet how to channel that in a way that would improve my health instead of cause it to deteriorate.

My energy, confidence, and health began to erode. In chiropractic college, I decided to make my own nutrition a priority in my life, with my future husband's support. I started experimenting with cooking and foods, and soon found that every aspect of my life improved. I then started to help others. In my first year of practice, I was consulting with dozens of patients each month, many of whom were having the same struggles I had.

Most of their questions were the same. How can I make food that tastes great, keeps me full, and makes me healthy? What can I make that my family will actually eat? How can I do this on a budget? What if I'm not ready to go completely grain free and sugar free? With those questions in mind, I compiled a self-published cookbook, Alive, in 2012. The demand for a follow-up book was so apparent that I began compiling the pages that you hold in your hand.

I know the recipes taste great because I've tried them, and even put them through the ultimate test of whether a three-year-old and a picky husband will eat it. No matter where you are in this journey, I want you to live to your optimal potential, and I know that improving your nutrition is a key part of that!

With love,
Dr. Allison Kloss

My Favorites

Appliances

Commercial Blender: this is a versatile tool that I use every day! I make smoothies, dips, soups, and sauces with it because it is powerful, reliable, and easy to clean up.

Professional Grade Stand Mixer: I use mine to mix cookies, pancakes, waffles, cakes, or anything that has a batter. It creates a consistent texture and mixes the ingredients well. The more you cook, the more time it will save you!

Food Processor: This is great for making hummus, nut butters, chicken salads, and nut bars. I use mine 2–3 times a week.

Food Dehydrator: This is great for making yogurt, jerky, fruit leathers, or dried fruit. My family loves dried apple rings! My daughter takes a fruit leather to school every day for her snack.

Manual Food Chopper: I use this often to chop nuts, veggies, and especially salsa. It's a great alternative to the blender if you like things chopped chunkier.

Slow Cooker: This is great for work days when I'm away all day because I just put the ingredients in before I leave, and by dinner time, it is ready. It can also be started before you go to bed so breakfast is ready when you wake up.

Pressure Cooker: I recently added this appliance to my kitchen, and it has absolutely wowed me! It does what my slow cooker does, but it gets the job done in minutes. I make hard boiled eggs in it every week and if you are like me and forget to set out your frozen meat, it can cook frozen chicken in 15 minutes. This is now my second favorite appliance.

Ice Cream Maker: I love ice cream, but I need to avoid the processed dairy and added sugar. I've found it's better and cheaper to just make my own! Since dairy really isn't much of an option for my oldest daughter and me, we stick with coconut milk ice cream.

Mandolin Slicer (Spiralizer): great for making veggie chips, veggie pasta, or sliced veggies for salads. Sweet potato chips are our favorite.

What About Sugar?

Natural Sugar Sources

Every day, I see the ill effects of processed sugar on my patients! It is addictive, causes weight gain, increases inflammation, and ruins people's confidence and health. My advice is to minimize your sugar use (even natural sugars) whenever possible!

I understand that most people will want some sugar in their diet, so I have outlined and included the best natural sources of sugar for you to use if you feel that you cannot eliminate it completely.

The Best Natural Sugars

The best natural sugars come from whole foods and include fiber. This includes bananas, dates, berries, apples, and most other fruits. While they still affect your blood sugar and should be eaten in moderation, the combination of sugar with fiber and other nutrients helps to slow sugar absorption and give you some added benefits.

The next best form of sugar is naturally occurring sugars, such as raw honey and organic maple syrup. These sugars are less processed because they are found in nature, and they tend to be less addictive than processed sugar.

The only sweetener or sugar substitute that I endorse is Stevia. The stevia plant is naturally occurring (I have grown my own Stevia plants before), and it will not affect your blood sugar. Using Stevia requires some practice, as it will ruin a dish if you use too much, but it can be worth it for when you want something sweet without the ill effects of sugar.

Flours for Baking and Cooking

Almond Flour is great for cakes, cupcakes, and crackers. However, because it is a nut, I have to be sensitive about where I take it.

Coconut Flour is a little trickier to bake with, but definitely not impossible. When I need to send food with my daughter to school this is my go to flour. I make the same things with it as I would with almond flour (cupcakes, muffins, etc.).

Chickpea/Garbanzo Flour is a dense flour with an unexpectedly light texture. This flour is great for batters to fry chicken or fish in, and for flatbreads (but it isn't limited to those methods).

Buckwheat Flour is actually a pseudo-grain (similar to quinoa). This is a great option for those who want to be nut free and gluten free. It can be substituted for regular flour at a 1:1 ratio. I find this flour tends to be overpowering in taste, but it's is great in baked goods (e.g. muffins and pancakes).

Sprouted Spelt Flour is what I use when I'm going where healthy foods are a foreign concept. It is considered an ancient grain and has retained its hard outer hull, which protects the inner grain from pests and the elements, making it is easier to digest.

Guidelines to Live by When Choosing Food

While this cookbook should act as a guide to help you create delicious recipes, there are also some basic principles that you should internalize to help you make food-related decisions in the future. I have broken them down into "great to consume" and "avoid" categories for easy reference.

Avoid	Great to Consume
Overprocessed Grains	Fish
Refined Oils	Grass-fed Meats
Refined Sugars	Nuts and Seeds
Processed/Canned Foods	Healthy Oils ands Fats
	Fruit (especially low sugar fruits)
	Vegetables
	Fermented Foods
	Cultured Cheeses

Another guideline that I always recommend is prioritizing good quality meats. If you can only make one change, this is the one to start with. For instance, it is challenging to find bacon with no added sugar; you just have to be diligent and look for it.

Dirty Dozen and Clean Fifteen

(*Environmental Working Group Website)
www.ewg.org

As a mother and chiropractor, I have become increasingly concerned about the toxic chemicals that are used to produce our food. I have also noticed that most people have a tendency to eat the same types of foods week after week, so I felt it was important to include this list for your reference.

The dirty dozen are the products that you should always buy organic. They typically have little or thin skin and can absorb pesticides in large doses.

I understand that every family must work within their budget when buying groceries, and the clean fifteen are foods that you can buy conventionally if you are concerned about the financial burden of buying organic foods. These foods often have a strong outer peel or shell, and/or they may not be commonly grown using harmful pesticides.

Must Buy Organic	Doesn't Need to Be Organic
Strawberries	Broccoli
Spinach	Avocado
Apples	Onions
Celery	Eggplant
Grapes	Cabbage
Pears	Mangoes
Nectarines	Sweet Peas
Peaches	Kiwi
Cherries	Asparagus
Bell Peppers	Pineapple
Tomatoes	Honeydews
Potatoes	Cauliflower
	Cantaloupe
	Papayas
	Sweet Corn

Refrigerator/Freezer Essentials

Dairy/Non Dairy

Coconut Milk

Almond Milk

Raw Milk

Raw Cheeses

Sour Cream

Cream Cheese

Homemade Yogurt

Eggs

Condiments

Ketchup

Mustard

Mayonnaise

Nut Butter

Coconut Aminos

Homemade Jam

Homemade Ranch

Hummus

Drinks

Kombucha

Lemon and Lime Juice

Sparkling Water

Freezer Essentials

Frozen Berries

Frozen Bananas

Organic Meats

Frozen Veggies

Homemade Popsicles

Pantry Essentials

I believe that keeping your pantry well stocked is a key ingredient for cooking well at home! If you decide to make a recipe at the last minute, but you are missing one or two ingredients, it can be incredibly difficult.

Flours
Coconut	Almond	Chickpea/Garbanzo Flour	Sprouted Spelt

Sweeteners
Stevia (the purest form is green)	Raw Honey	Pure Maple Syrup
Coconut Sugar	Organic Cane Sugar	

Oils
Extra Virgin Olive Oil (cold pressed)	Unrefined Coconut Oil	Avocado Oil
Sesame Oil	Macadamia Nut Oil	

Nuts and Seeds
Almonds	Cashews	Pecans	Walnuts
Pumpkin Seeds	Sunflower	Chia Seeds	Flaxseed
Sesame	Quinoa		

Dried Fruits
Cranberries	Raisins	Goji Berries	Golden Berries

Baking Needs
Baking Soda and Powder (aluminum free)	Unsweetened Shredded Coconut	Raw Cocoa Powder
Unsweetened Carob Chips	Arrowroot Powder	Baker's Chocolate
Vanilla Extract		

Beans and Other
Dried Beans	Lentils	Red Lentil/Black Bean Pasta

Other
Protein Powder (sweetened with stevia)	Grass-Fed Gelatin	Rolled Oats

If you are starting from scratch, it will help to budget an extra $10–15 per week to begin stocking up on all of these essentials. They will not go bad, and can be used in a variety of different recipes. I recommend storing nuts and nut flours in the refrigerator or freezer.

Traveling Inspirations

Since meeting my husband, he has ignited my love to travel. There's something mesmerizing about indulging in the culture and cuisine of other countries. I often look at a map and dream of to amazing variety of foods the world has to offer.

My first big trip outside of North America was to Vietnam while I was still in chiropractic school for an international clinical work study. I was amazed at the peace in that country, and the food was delicious. Everything was fresh, there was always an abundance of vegetables, and while learning the process of preparing a salad roll I realized how rewarding it is to learn a completely new recipe. I wanted to teach everyone else I knew back home how to make it as well! My journey towards this cookbook had begun…

Since then, we have tried foods in Thailand, Czech Republic, Hungary, England, and France. In each place I learned something new, and I have done my best to bring my favorite recipes and ideas, make them as healthy and tasty as possible, and deliver them to you in a way that is affordable and easy to make.

Smoothies

Wild Berry Smoothie

Prep Time: 5 minutes

Gluten free, grain free, dairy free   *Serves: 2-3*

This is my family's "go to" smoothie. I have made this probably over a thousand times and it tastes different every time

Directions

1. Add all ingredients in the order listed.
2. Blend.
3. Add water until it reaches your ideal consistency.

Ingredients

1 cup frozen berries (blueberries, raspberries, or strawberries)
Handful of ice
½ cup spinach
2 tablespoons chia seeds
1 tablespoon flax seed
¼ cup coconut milk
¾ cup or more of water
½ teaspoon cinnamon
1 scoop protein powder (check ingredients, should only be sweetened with stevia)

Old-fashioned Chocolate Shake

(Dr. Tom Recipe)

Prep Time: 5 minutes

Serves: 2-3

This chocolate shake recipe tastes like a milkshake you would get at an old-fashioned ice cream shop!

Directions

1. Add all ingredients in order listed.
2. Blend.
3. Add water until it reaches your ideal consistency.

Ingredients

1 cup coconut or almond milk

1 scoop chocolate grass-fed whey protein powder

1 frozen banana (or regular banana with a couple of ice cubes)

Splash of organic vanilla extract

1-2 teaspoon of unsweetened cocoa powder

1 tablespoon of raw almond butter (organic if possible)

Optional: chia seeds

Green Machine Smoothie

Prep Time: 5 minutes

Serves: 2-3

Directions

1. Add all ingredients in the order listed.
2. Blend.
3. Add water until it reaches your ideal consistency.

Ingredients

1 cup frozen unsweetened peach slices
1 cup packed kale or spinach, stems discarded
1/2 frozen banana
3/4 cup coconut water
1/2 teaspoon freshly grated ginger
½ avocado, deseeded

Pumpkin Pie Smoothie

Prep Time: 5 minutes

Serves: 2-3

Directions

1. Add all ingredients to your blender in the order in which they are listed above.
2. Blend.
3. Add water until the smoothie reaches your preferred consistency.

Ingredients

¼ cup mashed pumpkin

1 banana, frozen

1 cup unsweetened almond or coconut milk

2 tablespoons almond or cashew butter

1½ teaspoon vanilla

1 teaspoon cinnamon (or more, to taste)

½ teaspoon nutmeg

½ cup crushed ice cubes

Optional: 1 scoop vanilla protein powder

Refreshing Mango Lasse

Prep Time: 5 minutes

Serves: 2

Inspired by a street vendor in Thailand.

Directions

1. Add all ingredients to your blender in the order in which they are listed above.
2. Blend.
3. Add water until the smoothie reaches your preferred consistency.

Ingredients

1 cup mango (fresh or frozen)
3 ice cubes
1 scoop vanilla protein
½ teaspoon cinnamon
handful of parsley
¾ cup homemade almond or coconut milk

Fresh Berry Punch

Prep Time: 5 minutes

Serves: 2-3

This is a great alternative to classic punch. I have served this at many parties.

Directions

1. Blend all the ingredients until smooth, and pour through a strainer if desired.
2. Serve chilled.

*I recommend pouring this over ice to give it an even more refreshing feel.

Ingredients

1 cup blackberries
1 cup blueberries
1 cup raspberries
1 teaspoon honey
5 cups water or sparkling water

Breakfast

Grainless Granola

Prep Time: 5 –10 minutes

Grain free, sugar free, gluten free, dairy free   *Serves: 6–8*

I often give this as a gift by putting it in a mason jar with a bow around it. It is a great alternative to standard oat granola.

Directions

1. Toss all ingredients together.
2. You can either bake on a cookie sheet at 300°F for 15 minutes or keep it raw.
3. Serve with berries and yogurt.

Ingredients

2 cups almonds, chopped or sliced
1 cup pecans, chopped
1 cup cashews, chopped
½ cup dried cranberries
1/2 cup coconut flakes
¼ cup hemp seeds
¼ cup coconut oil, melted
5 tablespoons flaxseed meal
1 teaspoon cinnamon
1 teaspoon vanilla
A few drops of liquid stevia, depending on taste

Loaded Veggie Frittata

Prep Time: 20 minutes
Bake Time: 40 minutes

Grain free, sugar free, gluten free, dairy free   *Serves: 6*

This is a staple in my house! I make this on Sundays so breakfast is ready for up to 2–3 days. You can always put ground meat or cooked sausages in this to give it more of a protein punch, and it will definitely keep you full until lunch.

Directions

1. Preheat oven to 350°F.
2. Grease a 9" round pan with coconut oil and line the bottom and sides with sweet potatoes (you will need to overlap the sweet potatoes, because they do shrink).
3. Place the pan in the oven for about 20 minutes, or until the sweet potatoes are soft.
4. While your sweet potatoes are cooking, sauté the vegetables in a skillet with coconut oil (remember that the spinach will shrink significantly).
5. While the veggies are cooking, whisk eggs, coconut milk, and salt and pepper in a bowl.
6. Once the veggies are soft, arrange them in an even layer on top of the sweet potato crust. Then pour the egg mixture over top.
7. At this point, you can add organic shredded cheese. (To keep it dairy free, add ¼ cup of nutritional yeast to the top. If you use nutritional yeast, mix it in with the eggs before pouring them into the pan.)
8. Place in the oven and bake for 20–25 minutes, or until firm in the middle. Depending on how hot your oven is, you might want to check on the frittata after 10 minutes to see how it is cooking. It should not be runny in the middle.
9. Remove from oven and let cool for 15 minutes.

Ingredients

8–10 eggs
1 sweet potato (thinly sliced)
½ onion, chopped
1 cup mushrooms, chopped
3 cups spinach, chopped
2 tablespoons coconut oil
½ cup coconut milk
¼ cup nutritional yeast or organic shredded cheese
Sea salt and pepper, to taste

Traditional Breakfast Sausage Patties

Prep Time: 5 –10 minutes
Bake Time: 23 minutes

Grain free, sugar free, gluten free, dairy free   *Serves: 2–4*

Directions

1. Measure and mix spices.
2. Add spices to ground beef and mix together with hands.
3. Form and cook the sausages:
   - For mini sausage balls, roll into 24 balls of equal size and place each one in a mini muffin tin. Bake at 350°F for 20–23 minutes, or until no longer pink in the center.
   - For sausage patties, form into 12 patties of equal size. Pan fry the sausages in a cast iron skillet on medium-high heat, 3–4 minutes per side or until no longer pink in the center.

Ingredients

1 pound ground beef or ground turkey
1 teaspoon sea salt
1 teaspoon sage
1 teaspoon thyme
1 teaspoon paprika
1 teaspoon black pepper
1/2 teaspoon cayenne pepper
1/2 teaspoon nutmeg

Homestyle Biscuits and Gravy

Prep Time: 15 minutes
Bake Time: 20 minutes

Sugar free, dairy free   *Serves: 2–4*

When I was living in Canada, it was hard to find biscuits and gravy, and even when I found them, they included white flour and sugar. It took me many attempts to figure out this recipe.

Gravy

Directions

1. Sprinkle flour over browned sausage. Pour 1/2 cup almond milk over the sausage mixture and stir.
2. Pour remaining 1/2 cup almond milk and observe the gravy's consistency (if you like thicker gravy, add less milk, and if you like thinner, add more).
3. Salt to taste.

*Note that the gravy will thicken slightly as it cools.

Ingredients

1 batch of browned breakfast sausage patties (cut up into pieces)
¼ cup spelt flour
1 cup almond milk (divided)
Salt to taste

Biscuits

Directions

1. Preheat oven to 450°F.
2. Slice chilled butter into 1/2" slices and place in blender or food processor.
3. Add flour, salt, and baking powder to the blender and pulse about 10 times until butter is incorporated.
4. Place flour mixture into a medium bowl and set aside. In a separate small bowl, whisk egg and water together.
5. Add liquid mixture to dry and stir until just combined.
6. Using a spoon and your hands, form six biscuits on a parchment-lined baking sheet.
7. Bake in preheated oven for 10–14 minutes. Check them at 10 min and slice one open. If it's still a little wet inside, bake for another 2–3 minutes. (Don't overcook!).

Ingredients

Ingredients
1 1/2 cups spelt flour
3 teaspoons baking powder
1/4 teaspoon salt
1 egg
1/2 cup water
½ cup butter or ghee, chilled

Cranberry Lemon Scone

Prep Time: 5 –10 minutes
Bake Time: 25 minutes (plus 10 minutes cooling)

Grain free, dairy free

Serves: 4

I often make this for brunch.

Scones

Directions

1. Preheat oven to 350°F. Grease a round baking dish with coconut oil.
2. Mix all ingredients.
3. Roll batter into a ball and place it on the baking dish.
4. Flatten the dough into a circle.
5. Place in the oven and cook for about 25 minutes.
6. Remove from oven and drizzle coconut icing on top.
7. Let sit for 10 minutes before serving.

Ingredients

2 cups almond flour
1 teaspoon baking soda
1/2 teaspoon sea salt
4 tablespoons lemon zest
2 teaspoons lemon juice
1 egg
4 tablespoons honey or maple syrup
½ cup cranberries, dried and unsweetened

Coconut Icing

Directions

1. Mix all ingredients in a saucepan
2. Lightly heat until all is mixed together.
3. Drizzle over scone.

**If you don't have coconut butter on hand you can use shredded coconut in the food processor.

Ingredients

3 tablespoons coconut butter*
4 tablespoons coconut milk
2 tablespoons honey

Almond Meal and Berry Pancakes

Prep Time: 15–20 minutes

Grain free, sugar free, gluten free, dairy free   *Serves: 2–3 (makes about 6 pancakes)*

My 3-year-old loves these pancakes!

Directions

1. Blend all ingredients in a blender. If the batter is too thick, you can add a tablespoon of coconut milk.
2. Heat skillet on stovetop with coconut oil or butter.
3. Spoon a tablespoon of batter onto the skillet.
4. Wait until the pancake bubbles, then flip the pancake.
5. Serve when golden brown.

Ingredients

2/3 cup almond meal

2 eggs

¼ cup raspberries or blueberries

½ teaspoon baking soda

Splash of vanilla

Dash of cinnamon

Drop of liquid stevia

Simple Waffles

Prep Time: 5–10 minutes
Bake Time: 5 minutes

Sugar free, dairy free   *Serves: 2–4*

My daughter would eat these with her eggs every morning if I let her. Sometimes I make a double batch of these and freeze a few for later.

Directions

1. Preheat your waffle maker.
2. In a medium bowl, whisk eggs, milk, and vanilla together.
3. Add flour, baking powder, cinnamon, and salt to the bowl and mix until all ingredients are combined.
4. Pour into your waffle maker. (My waffle maker usually takes 4 minutes.)
5. Let cool and serve with jam or pure maple syrup.

Ingredients

2 eggs
1 1/2 cups coconut milk
½ teaspoon vanilla
2 1/4 cups spelt flour
1 tablespoon baking powder
¼ teaspoon salt
1 teaspoon cinnamon

Jam-Packed Energy Bites

Prep Time: 20 minutes
Wait Time: 30 minutes

Grain free, sugar free, gluten free, dairy free   *Serves: 2–4*

These are great for traveling or for something to have on the go.

Directions

1. Preheat oven to 300°F.
2. Toast coconut, almonds, and pecans on cookie sheet until lightly brown. Take out of oven.
3. Place coconut, almonds, and pecans into a blender or food processor and chop until coarsely ground.
4. In a medium-sized bowl, combine almond flour, pumpkin seeds, and scoop of protein powder and toasted nut mix.
5. Melt almond butter, coconut oil, sea salt, and vanilla (if not using protein powder) in a saucepan.
6. Mix wet to dry.
7. Press into an 8" × 8" parchment-lined loaf pan.
8. Refrigerate until firm—about half an hour.
9. Cut into bars.

Ingredients

1/2 cup slivered almonds
1/2 cup pecans
1/4 cup pumpkin seeds
1/4 cup almond flour
1/4 cup unsweetened coconut
1 scoop vanilla protein powder (can substitute ½ teaspoon vanilla)
1/4 cup almond butter, or any nut butter
1/2 cup coconut oil
1/4 teaspoon sea salt
1/2 cup dried berries like golden berries, goji berries, unsweetened tart cherries

Spelt Blueberry Muffins

Prep Time: 5–10 minutes
Wait Time: 15 minutes

Dairy free   *Serves: 6*

These muffins never last long in my house. I usually quadruple the recipe and freeze a dozen.

Directions

1. Preheat oven to 350°F. Line a muffin pan with cupcake liners (or grease it).
2. Mix all dry ingredients together in a large mixing bowl.
3. In a separate bowl, mix the wet ingredients. Then add them to the dry ingredients.
4. Carefully fold in the blueberries, making sure to not over-mix the batter or break the blueberries.
5. Pour batter into muffin pan and bake for 12–15 minutes.
6. Let muffins cool before removing them from the pan.

Ingredients

1 cup spelt flour
1/2 teaspoon baking powder
1/4 teaspoon sea salt
Dash of cinnamon
1/4 cup coconut or almond milk
1 teaspoon apple cider vinegar
1/4 teaspoon vanilla extract
1/3 cup raw honey (can also use pure maple syrup)
3 1/2 tablespoons avocado oil (olive oil is too strong)
1/2 cup blueberries, frozen or fresh

Snacks

Cheese Ball

Prep Time: 5–10 minutes

Grain free, sugar free, gluten free   *Serves: 6–8*

When I was growing up, I would always find a cheese ball at the appetizer table during every major holiday. During the winter months, I make three cheese balls of decreasing size and use them to form a snowman.

Directions

1. Let cream cheese stand at room temperature until soft.
2. Mix all ingredients together using a spatula.
3. Divide into two balls.
4. Roll in chopped pecans.
5. Refrigerate.
6. Serve at room temperature with veggies or homemade crackers.

Ingredients

2 cups organic cream cheese
2 cups organic mozzarella cheese, shredded
1 teaspoon ground garlic
2 tablespoons coconut aminos or tamari
1 cup pecans, finely chopped

Warm Goat Cheese Dip

Prep Time: 5–10 minutes
Wait Time: 20 minutes

Grain free, sugar free, gluten free   *Serves: 4–6*

Directions

1. Preheat oven to 400ºF.
2. Spread avocado oil on a small baking dish.
3. Mix all ingredients and add to the greased dish.
4. Bake for 15–20 minutes or until bubbly.
5. Remove from oven and let cool for 10 minutes.
6. Serve with veggies or homemade crackers.

Ingredients

1/2 cup goat cheese, softened
1/2 cup organic cream cheese, softened
2 tablespoons balsamic vinegar
1/4 cup organic parmesan cheese
Sea salt and pepper to taste
2 tablespoons avocado oil

Guacamole

Prep Time: 5–10 minutes

Grain free, sugar free, gluten free, dairy free　　*Serves: 4–6*

Everyone loves guacamole. It's another great dip for veggies or crackers. I sometimes put this on salad as a dressing or right over some chicken-stuffed sweet potatoes.

Directions

1. Mix all ingredients together.
2. Serve with homemade crackers or veggie sticks.

Ingredients

2 ripe avocados, pitted
1 lime, squeezed
2 cloves garlic, minced
1 teaspoon sea salt
1/2–1 teaspoon ground cumin
1/2 teaspoon cilantro
1/4 onion, chopped
1/2 tomato, chopped

Roasted Red Pepper Hummus

Prep Time: 5–10 minutes

Grain free, sugar free, gluten free, dairy free　　*Serves: 4–6*

Directions

1. Place all ingredients in a food processor and process until smooth.
2. Store in a glass container (it keeps 5–7 days).
3. Serve with sliced veggies.

Ingredients

1 large can chickpeas (rinsed and drained)
4 chunks of roasted red pepper
1 garlic clove
3 tablespoons olive oil
2 tablespoons lemon juice (freshly squeezed)
1/2 teaspoon sea salt
Cayenne pepper (optional for spice)

Zucchini Bruschetta

Prep Time: 5–10 minutes
Wait Time: 6 minutes

Grain free, sugar free, gluten free   *Serves: 6–8*

I love how festive these look, and they are a better alternative than the traditional white flour ones.

Directions

1. Preheat oven to 375°F.
2. Mix tomatoes, basil, olive oil, balsamic vinegar, sea salt, and black pepper in a bowl.
3. Set tomato mixture aside to let flavors combine.
4. Cut zucchini into 1/4-inch-thick round slices.
5. Place zucchini slices on a baking sheet coated with olive oil.
6. Lightly brush zucchini slices with olive oil.
7. Bake in the oven for two minutes.
8. Flip zucchini slices, lightly coat with olive oil, and cook for two more minutes. Zucchini should be firm, not mushy.
9. Spoon tomato mixture on top of each zucchini slice and then top with cheese, if using.
10. Return to oven and bake for two more minutes.

Ingredients

6–7 Roma tomatoes, diced

2 garlic cloves, minced

8–12 basil leaves, stacked, rolled and cut into very thin slices

1 tablespoon olive oil + scant amount to brush on zucchini slices

1 teaspoon balsamic vinegar

1/4 teaspoon sea salt

1/8 teaspoon black pepper

1 large zucchini

1/4 cup organic shredded cheese

Trail Mix

Prep Time: 5–10 minutes

Grain free, sugar free, gluten free, dairy free   *Serves: 8–10*

This is great to keep in your purse or take with you when traveling.

Directions

1. Mix all ingredients together.
2. Store in a glass container.

Ingredients

1 cup walnuts
1 cup sliced almonds
1/4 cup dried cranberries
1/4 cup golden berries
1/2 cup dried apples, chopped
1/2 cup dried mango or other fruit
1 teaspoon cinnamon
Dash of sea salt
1/4 cup chocolate chips (sugar free)

Mango Salsa

Prep Time: 10 minutes

Grain free, sugar free, gluten free, dairy free   *Serves: 4–6*

Directions

1. Remove the skin from the mango and jicama.
2. Chop mango, jicama, peppers, and onion.
3. Add lime juice, sea salt, and chili powder.
4. Make sure the texture is chopped and resembles salsa.
5. Serve with veggies or homemade crackers.

Ingredients

1 large mango
1/2 small jicama
1/3 yellow bell pepper
1/3 red bell pepper
1 jalapeno pepper, stemmed
1/3 small red onion
1 tablespoon fresh lime juice
1/4 teaspoon sea salt
1/2 teaspoon chili powder

Apple Nachos

Prep Time: 5–10 minutes

Grain free, sugar free, gluten free, dairy free   *Serves: 2–4*

Directions

1. Slice the apples thin enough so it would be easy to eat the slice in one or two bites. I use my mandolin slicer, and it works great.
2. Spritz the apples with lemon juice to help prevent them from browning.
3. Melt sunflower seed butter and ghee in a small pot on low heat.
4. Drizzle it all over the apples.
5. Top the apples and sunflower seed butter with flaked coconut, sliced almonds, a few pecans, and chocolate chips.

Ingredients

3 crispy granny smith apples, cored
2 teaspoons lemon juice
¼ cup sunflower seed butter
1–2 tablespoon ghee
Sliced almonds
Pecans
Flaked unsweetened coconut
Chocolate chips (sugar free)

Curry Dip

Prep Time: 5–10 minutes

Grain free, sugar free, gluten free, dairy free   *Serves: 2–4*

When I'm hosting, I like to offer an option that isn't the typical ranch dip or hummus.

Directions

1. Mix all ingredients together.
2. Store in the refrigerator. This keeps for 5–7 days.

Ingredients

1 teaspoon grated onion
1 teaspoon apple cider vinegar
1 teaspoon garlic salt
1 teaspoon curry powder
1 teaspoon horseradish
1 cup vegenaise or homemade mayo

Stuffed Dates

Prep Time: 5–10 minutes

Grain free, sugar free, gluten free   *Serves: 2–4*

Directions

1. Mix ingredients—except dates—together to make a cream filling.
2. Stuff the dates with cream filling.

Ingredients

12 Medjool dates, pitted
1/2 cup organic cream cheese or 1/2 cup goat cheese
2 tablespoons coconut milk
Herb mix (1 teaspoon each oregano, cumin, parsley)

Salads

Cucumber and Chicken Salad Sandwiches

Prep Time: 15 minutes

Grain free, sugar free, gluten free, dairy free   *Serves: 2–4*

These are great to serve at a bridal or baby shower.

Directions

1. Cook the chicken however you like. I usually boil it in water on the stovetop.
2. While the chicken is cooking, place the celery in the food processor and pulse 2–3 times.
3. Add cooked chicken to the rest of the ingredients and process until the consistency is uniform.
4. Spread chicken salad between two slices of cucumber.

Ingredients

2 English cucumbers, sliced into thick rounds

For the chicken salad:
2 cups shredded chicken, cooked
3 celery hearts
½ cup homemade mayonnaise or grapeseed vegenaise
Salt and pepper to taste

Egg Salad

(Dr. Tom Recipe)

Prep Time: 10 minutes

Grain free, sugar free, gluten free, dairy free   *Serves: 5–6*

Directions

1. Chop boiled eggs.
2. Gently mix all ingredients together.
3. Serve in lettuce boats or as a dip for your favorite veggie sticks.

Ingredients

6–8 hard-boiled eggs
2–3 stalks celery, chopped
1/4 red onion, chopped
1–2 tablespoon spicy deli mustard
1 teaspoon paprika
1 cup homemade mayonnaise or vegenaise

Bacon and Garbanzo Bean Salad

Prep Time: 15 minutes

Grain free, sugar free, gluten free   *Serves: 4*

Directions

1. To make the dressing, stir mayonnaise, cheese, lemon juice, basil, and salt and pepper together in a small bowl.
2. In a large bowl, toss remaining ingredients except the lettuce together.
3. Gently mix in the dressing.
4. Cover; refrigerate at least 1 hour to blend flavors.
5. Line the serving dish with lettuce.
6. Spoon the salad over lettuce.
7. Sprinkle with additional sunflower seeds and parmesan cheese, if desired.

Ingredients

1/2 cup mayonnaise
1/2 cup Parmesan cheese, freshly grated (can omit or add 1/4 cup nutritional yeast instead)
2 tablespoons lemon juice
1 tablespoon fresh basil, chopped
1/4 teaspoon salt
1/8 teaspoon pepper, coarsely ground
6 slices bacon, cooked and coarsely chopped
2 cups garbanzo beans, drained and rinsed
1/2 cup red onion, coarsely chopped
1/4 cup sunflower seeds
Lettuce leaves, if desired

Broccoli and Cauliflower Salad

Prep Time: 10 minutes

Grain free, sugar free, gluten free   *Serves: 4–6*

You can add some protein like chicken breast to make this a complete meal.

Directions

1. Chop cauliflower and broccoli into small florets (1/2 inch).
2. Add onion, parsley, and remaining ingredients
3. Stir in vegenaise, mustard, and salt.

Ingredients

1 head cauliflower

1 head broccoli

1 small onion, finely chopped (about 3–4 tablespoons)

1 cup shredded organic cheese or ½ cup nutritional yeast

1 tablespoons parsley, finely chopped

1/2 cup pumpkin seeds

1/4 cup unsweetened dried cranberries

2 tablespoons grapeseed oil vegenaise, or homemade mayonnaise

1 tablespoon Dijon mustard

1/2 teaspoon sea salt

Magical Shredded Kale Salad

(Dr. Tom Recipe)

Prep Time: 5–10 minutes

Grain free, sugar free, gluten free, dairy free   *Serves: 2–4*

Shredding kale is a game-changer! It takes away the toughness and makes it magical! Play with the amounts of all the dry ingredients to suit your tastes.

Directions

1. Clean the kale and shred it in a food processor.
2. Mix all dry ingredients.
3. Add olive oil and balsamic vinegar to taste.

Ingredients

12 cups kale
1/2 cup goat cheese
4 tablespoons olive oil
2 tablespoons balsamic vinegar
1/2–1 granny smith apple, diced
¼ cup red onion, chopped
¼ cup dried cranberries or strawberries
Salt and pepper to taste
Chopped pecans (optional)

Lemon Kale Parmesan Salad

Prep Time: 5–10 minutes

Grain free, sugar free, gluten free   *Serves: 2–4*

Directions

1. Clean the kale and shred it in a food processor.
2. Squeeze lemon for juice.
3. Mix all ingredients in a large bowl.

Ingredients

2 cups kale shredded
1 lemon
¼ cup parmesan cheese fine grated
2 teaspoon smoked paprika
1/8 cup pine nuts
Grilled chicken (optional)

Summer Fruit Salad

Prep Time: 5–10 minutes

Grain free, sugar free, gluten free, dairy free   *Serves: 2–4*

Directions

1. Dice strawberries, pineapples, and mangos.
2. Mix all the fruit in a bowl.
3. Drizzle with 2 tablespoons of lemon juice and stir.

Ingredients

1 cup blueberries
1/2 cup raspberries
1 cup strawberries, diced
1/2 cup pineapple, diced
1 cup mango, diced
2 tablespoons lemon juice

"Macaroni" Salad

(Dr. Tom Recipe)

Prep Time: 5–10 minutes

Grain free, sugar free, gluten free, dairy free   *Serves: 2–4*

This healthy macaroni salad is quick and delicious!

Directions

1. Cook lentil pasta according to the package directions.
2. Rinse with cold water and drain.
3. Add all ingredients together in a big bowl and mix gently.
4. Refrigerate in a covered bowl to allow all the flavors to soak in.

Ingredients

1 box red lentil rotini pasta
3 hard boiled eggs, chopped
1 small red onion, diced
1 green bell pepper, diced
3/4 cup celery, diced
1 cup homemade mayonnaise or vegenaise
1/4 cup spicy brown mustard
Salt and pepper to taste

Soups

Black Bean Soup

Prep Time: 15 minutes
Wait Time: 40 minutes

Grain free, sugar free, gluten free, dairy free   *Serves: 2–4*

This soup is packed with dense nutrients, and it will not leave you hungry after one bowl. My daughter loves this, and I sometimes add some chickpea noodles to her bowl. This can be served over quinoa or riced cauliflower.

Directions

1. Wash the beans; pick out and discard the ones that are floating to the top. Place the remaining beans in a large pot and add the water.
2. Heat to boil.
3. Remove from the heat and cover for 1 hour.
4. Heat oil in a Dutch oven and sauté onion, garlic, and celery for 5 minutes.
5. Add allspice, stock, and bay leaf.
6. Drain beans and add to Dutch oven.
7. Bring to a boil and simmer for 2–4 hours.
8. Add the apples and meat to the soup for the last 30 minutes of cooking.

Ingredients

1 pound dried black beans
6 cups filtered water
2 tablespoons extra virgin olive oil
2 celery hearts, chopped
1 onion, chopped
4 garlic cloves, minced
2 teaspoons allspice
3 1/2 cups organic beef or chicken stock
1 bay leaf
2 granny smith apples, cored and diced
1 pound beef sausage, cut into 2-inch pieces (optional)

Vibrant Broccoli Soup

Prep Time: 15 minutes
Wait Time: 20 minutes

Grain free, sugar free, gluten free   *Serves: 2–4*

Directions

1. Bring a stock pot half filled with water to a boil. Add sea salt and broccoli florets.
2. Place lid on the pot and boil for 5 minutes.
3. Drain broccoli and reserve the liquid.
4. Place cooked broccoli in the blender with a pinch of sea salt until the blender is almost full. Add 1 ½ cups of the reserved broccoli liquid.
5. Blend until the mixture is smooth. Add the rest of the broccoli and puree.
6. Place the mixture back in the stock pot and add coconut milk, butter, and chicken stock. Place on low heat until heated through.
7. Add whatever seasoning you would like, to taste.

Ingredients

Fresh broccoli, 6 small bunches
1 can coconut milk, full fat
1 teaspoon sea salt
1 tablespoon butter or ghee
1/2–1 cup chicken stock

Butternut Squash Soup

Prep Time: 30 minutes
Wait Time: 40 minutes

Grain free, sugar free, gluten free, dairy free   *Serves: 6–8*

Directions

1. Peel, clean, and de-seed butternut squash.
2. In a bowl, rub clove and nutmeg over squash with a little bit of oil.
3. Roast squash in oven at 350°F for 20 minutes (until soft).
4. While squash is roasting, heat a pot and sauté onions, carrots, and garlic.
5. Add chicken stock and cinnamon to the sautéed vegetables.
6. Scoop out the cooked butternut squash into the stock mixture once it is removed from the oven.
7. Bring to a boil, and then simmer for 30 minutes.
8. Blend to a smooth puree.
9. Add coconut milk and stir well.
10. Taste and season with more salt and pepper if needed.

Ingredients

1 butternut squash
1 onion, chopped
2 carrots, chopped
1 zucchini, peeled and chopped
1 garlic clove
2 cups chicken stock
1 cup water or more chicken stock
1 cup coconut milk
1 teaspoon nutmeg
1/2 teaspoon ground clove
Sea salt and ground black pepper, to taste
1 tablespoon cinnamon

Easy Carrot and Ginger Soup

Prep Time: 5–10 minutes
Wait Time: 25 minutes

Grain free, sugar free, gluten free, dairy free   *Serves: 2–4*

This dish always brings me back to memories of my favorite Manitoba deli.

Directions

1. Melt butter with the first 7 ingredients in the pot for 8 minutes.
2. Place stock and milk in pot and bring to a boil.
3. Simmer until carrots are soft, usually 20–30 minutes.
4. Blend until smooth.

Ingredients

7 carrots, chopped
1 onion, chopped
1 tablespoon garlic, minced
3 tablespoons ginger, minced
1 1/2 teaspoon sea salt
1 teaspoon ground pepper
2 teaspoon turmeric
2 cups chicken stock
2 cups coconut milk
2 tablespoons butter or ghee

Cream of Mushroom Soup

Prep Time: 5–10 minutes
Wait Time: 20 minutes

Sugar free, dairy free   *Serves: 2–4*

This freezes well in ice cube trays and is nice to have on cold days or just to mix with chicken or serve on top of a steak. Use immediately or store in the refrigerator in an airtight container.

Directions

1. In a bowl, whisk milk and flour until all lumps are dissolved.
2. In a medium saucepan, bring the vegetable broth to a boil.
3. Add mushrooms and spices to the vegetable broth and stir to combine.
4. Add the milk/flour mixture to the broth, whisking to combine.
5. Reduce heat to medium, and continue to cook until thickened (3–5 minutes), stirring constantly.
6. Remove from heat.

Ingredients

3/4 cup finely chopped mushrooms
1/3 cup spelt flour
2/3 cup coconut milk
1 1/4 cup vegetable broth
1 teaspoon onion powder
1 teaspoon garlic powder
1/4 teaspoon celery salt
1/4 teaspoon salt
1/4 teaspoon pepper

Curry Lentil Soup

Prep Time: 5 – 10 minutes
Wait Time: 20 minutes

Grain free, sugar free, gluten free, dairy free   *Serves: 2–4*

Directions

1. Begin by heating a large pot on medium-high heat.
2. Add coconut oil to melt, and sauté ginger and garlic for 2–3 minutes.
3. Add lentils and broth and bring to a boil.
4. Reduce heat to medium.
5. Add curry powder and turmeric.
6. Let simmer for 10–15 minutes, until the lentils have soaked up most of the liquid and are soft.
7. Add coconut milk and stir until nice and creamy.

Ingredients

1 tablespoon coconut oil
1 tablespoon minced ginger
2 cloves garlic, minced
2 1/4 cups red lentils (rinsed)
6 cups chicken broth
1 teaspoon cayenne
2 tablespoons curry powder
2 teaspoons turmeric
Salt to taste
1 1/2 cups coconut milk

Roasted Red Pepper Soup

Prep Time: 5 minutes
Wait Time: 10 minutes

Grain free, sugar free, gluten free, dairy free   *Serves: 1*

If I have time, I usually roast the red pepper with a drizzle of avocado oil at 375°F for about 15 minutes, and then I add it to the blender. Either way, it tastes great!

Directions

1. Blend all ingredients together.
2. Warm on the stovetop.
3. Garnish with cilantro.

Ingredients

1 avocado
1 red pepper, deseeded
1 bunch cilantro
1/2 cup vegetable or chicken broth
1/4 cup coconut or nut milk
Salt and pepper to taste

Traditional Tomato Soup

Prep Time: 5–10 minutes
Wait Time: 10 minutes

Grain free, sugar free, gluten free, dairy free   *Serves: 1–2*

This is another basic soup that can be frozen in ice trays. It's perfect for those cooler autumn or winter days.

Directions

1. In a blender, purée all ingredients together.
2. Add more water if necessary.
3. Heat on stovetop for 10 minutes or desired temperature.

Ingredients

6 small Roma tomatoes
2 cups water
2 garlic cloves, roughly chopped
2 carrots, chopped

Cauliflower Sweet Potato Soup

Prep Time: 25 minutes
Wait Time: 30 minutes

Grain free, sugar free, gluten free, dairy free   *Serves: 2–4*

Directions

1. Preheat oven to 400°F.
2. Cut cauliflower into small pieces and roast on a baking sheet drizzled in olive oil for about 20 minutes.
3. While the cauliflower bakes, boil sweet potatoes in about 6 cups of water.
4. In a stock pot, sauté onion and garlic.
5. Once the sweet potatoes and cauliflower are done, add most of them to the pot, mix together, and sauté for about 5 minutes.
6. Let the soup cool, and then blend it in the blender until smooth.
7. Combine the reserved chunky vegetables with the blended mixture and stir.
8. Salt and pepper to taste.

Ingredients

1 large head of cauliflower
2 large sweet potatoes, cut in pieces
1 sweet onion, chopped
3 cloves garlic
Filtered water

Side Dishes

Sweet Potato Fries

Prep Time: 5–10 minutes
Wait Time: 25 minutes

Grain free, sugar free, gluten free, dairy free   *Serves: 2–3*

For more variety, you can always use a mandolin slicer and make "chips."

Directions

1. Preheat oven to 400°F.
2. Line a baking sheet with parchment paper.
3. Transfer the fries to a clean bowl. Toss with the olive oil, arrowroot powder, and seasoning, using your hands or a spoon to coat evenly.
4. Arrange the fries in a single layer on the lined baking sheet.
5. Bake at 400°F for 15 minutes.
6. After the 15 minutes, remove from the oven, flip them over using a fork, and then return the sheet to the oven for another 10 minutes, or until the fries are golden around the edges.
7. Sprinkle with sea salt and pepper immediately, while the fries are still hot and glossy.
8. Let cool for 5–10 minutes.

Ingredients

2 medium sweet potatoes, peeled and cut into fry shapes
4 tablespoons olive oil
2 teaspoons cinnamon
1 teaspoon garlic powder
Sea salt and pepper
Sprinkle of arrowroot powder

Vegetables in a Basket

Prep Time: 40 minutes
Wait Time: 25 minutes

Grain free, sugar free, gluten free, dairy free   *Serves: 4–6*

Perfect for those summer patio parties. I love making this when we grill out with some sirloin steaks and have dinner outside. Throw these veggies in a grill basket and grill until softened.

Directions

1. Let marinate for at least 30 minutes (the longer, the better).
2. Preheat oven to 350°F.
3. Bake for 20–25 minutes on a cookie sheet.

Ingredients

Veggies (broccoli, cauliflower, zucchini, summer squash, sweet potatoes), cut into bite-size pieces

Marinade
1/2 cup olive oil
1/2 cup apple cider vinegar
1/2 teaspoon garlic powder
1/2 teaspoon rosemary
1/2 teaspoon sea salt
1/4 teaspoon pepper

Baked Curry Cauliflower

Prep Time: 10–15 minutes
Wait Time: 45 minutes

Grain free, sugar free, gluten free, dairy free   *Serves: 4–6*

Directions

1. Preheat oven to 350°F.
2. In a bowl, toss cauliflower with oil until all florets are coated.
3. Sprinkle all the spices over the cauliflower and stir again.
4. Spread cauliflower in a glass baking dish and bake for 40–45 minutes.

Ingredients

4 cups cauliflower florets
3 tablespoons coconut oil
1 tablespoon curry powder
1 teaspoon garlic powder
1/4 teaspoon turmeric
Sea salt to taste

Roasted Sweet Potatoes and Brussels Sprouts

Prep Time: 20 minutes
Wait Time: 45 minutes

Grain free, sugar free, gluten free, dairy free   *Serves: 4–6*

Directions

1. Preheat oven to 400°F.
2. Trim your Brussels sprouts by cutting off the little brown end. If there are any yellow leaves, pull them off. Cut any large sprouts in half. Put sprouts in a large bowl.
3. Peel sweet potato and chop into 1–2 inch pieces. Add to the large bowl.
4. Mince 2 cloves of garlic and add it to the bowl.
5. Pour 1/3 cup avocado oil over the vegetables.
6. Add cumin, garlic salt, salt, and pepper to taste.
7. Stir to coat.
8. Drizzle a little avocado oil onto the sheet pan and rub it all over the pan with your hand.
9. Pour the veggies onto the pan.
10. Roast at 400ºF for about 40–45 minutes. The veggies are done when they are slightly brown and a fork slides into them easily.
11. Place the veggies in a serving bowl and toss with 1–2 tablespoons of red wine vinegar to taste.

Ingredients

1 pound Brussels sprouts, trimmed and halved
1 large sweet potato, diced
2 cloves garlic, minced
1/3 cup avocado oil
1 teaspoon cumin
1/4 or 1/2 teaspoon garlic salt
1 teaspoon salt
1 tablespoon red wine vinegar
Pepper to taste

Cheesy Cauliflower Patties

Prep Time: 20 minutes
Wait Time: 10 minutes

Grain free, sugar free, gluten free   *Serves: 4–6*

Directions

1. Cut cauliflower into florets and cook in boiling water until tender. Drain.
2. Mash the cauliflower while still warm.
3. Stir in cheese, eggs, almond flour, cayenne, and salt to taste.
4. Coat the bottom of a skillet with coconut oil over medium-high heat.
5. Form the cauliflower mixture into patties about 3 inches across.
6. Cook until golden brown and set, about 3 minutes per side.
7. Keep each batch warm in the oven while you cook the rest.

Ingredients

1 head cauliflower
2 large eggs
1/2 cup organic or raw cheese, grated
1/2 cup almond flour
1/2 teaspoon cayenne pepper
Salt
Coconut oil

Oven-Baked Zucchini Fritters

Prep Time: 20 minutes
Wait Time: 30 minutes

Grain free, sugar free, gluten free   *Serves: 4–6*

Another great way to hide some vegetables for toddlers. Optional: Serve hot with a dollop of sour cream on top.

Directions

1. Place grated zucchini in a strainer in the sink and add salt. Let sit for 10 minutes.
2. Using a clean dish towel or cheese cloth, drain zucchini completely.
3. In a large bowl, combine all ingredients except coconut oil.
4. Coat baking sheet with coconut oil.
5. Scoop tablespoons of batter for each fritter, flattening with a spatula.
6. Cook in the oven on 350°F for 10–15 minutes on each side.

Ingredients

4 cups shredded zucchini
2 eggs
2/3 cups coconut flour
1 teaspoon salt
1/3 cup organic parmesan cheese
2 cloves garlic, minced
2 tablespoons coconut oil

Onion Rings

Prep Time: 15 minutes
Wait Time: 20 minutes

Grain free, sugar free, gluten free, dairy free   *Serves: 2–4*

Directions

1. Crack eggs into a bowl.
2. Pour coconut flour and spice into a separate bowl and stir.
3. Heat the oil in a skillet on the stove.
4. Dredge each sliced onion ring in coconut flour, then eggs, then coconut flour again.
5. Drop covered rings into the hot oil to fry until golden brown and flip with tongs to brown other side.
6. Remove rings to a paper towel to dry.

Ingredients

Coconut flour
Onion, thinly sliced in rings
Coconut or avocado oil
1–2 eggs
Garlic powder
Pinch of cayenne pepper

Cold Veggie Pizza

Prep Time: 5-10 minutes

Grain free, sugar free, gluten free, dairy free　　*Serves: 4-6*

You could also make a crust for the bottom layer if you want using the quiche tart crust.

Directions

1. Mix all ingredients except for the veggies.
2. Spread on a large, flat platter.
3. Sprinkle all the chopped veggies on top.

Ingredients

1 1/2 cup organic cream cheese

2 tablespoons vegenaise or homemade mayo

2 tablespoons tamari or coconut aminos

1 small onion, grated

1 tablespoon lemon juice

1/2 teaspoon garlic powder

1/2 teaspoon onion powder

1 tablespoon dried parsley

Veggie toppings: 1 cup broccoli, cauliflower, carrots chopped

Quiche Tarts

Prep Time: 15 minutes
Wait Time: 30 minutes

Grain free, sugar free, gluten free

Serves: 8–10 (makes 24 tarts)

These freeze really well. Reheat at 350°F for 10 minutes.

Directions

Crust
1. Place almond flour and salt in the food processor and pulse briefly.
2. Add coconut oil and egg and pulse until mixture forms a ball.
3. Press dough into small muffin tins.
4. Bake tart shells at 350°F until crisp.

Filling
1. While the crust is cooking, mix the filling ingredients, making sure they are well blended.
2. Fill each tart, but not to overflowing.
3. Bake for 20 to 30 minutes at 375°F.
4. Cool for 10 minutes.
5. Remove from pan by going around each tart with a sharp knife. Let cool on a paper towel.

Ingredients

Crust:
2 cups blanched almond flour
1/2 teaspoon sea salt
2 tablespoon coconut oil
1 egg

Filling:
3/4 cup coconut milk
2 beaten eggs
1/4 cup finely chopped broccoli
1/4 cup chopped red peppers
3/4 cup shredded organic cheese

Stuffed Poppers

Prep Time: 20 minutes
Wait Time: 20 minutes

Grain free, sugar free, gluten free, dairy free   *Serves: 4–6*

These poppers can also be wrapped in bacon.

Directions

Cheese Sauce Directions
1. Soak cashews in water for 2–4 hours, rinse and drain.
2. Add all ingredients to a high-powered blender
3. Blend on high until super smooth, scraping sides as needed. You may add additional water one tablespoonful at a time to reach the desired consistency.

Stuffed Popper Directions
1. Preheat oven to 350°F.
2. Cut peppers in half lengthwise and deseed. I recommend wearing gloves while taking the seeds out.
3. Place in an 8" × 8" baking dish.
4. Spoon Cheese Sauce into peppers.
5. Bake for 20 minutes or until cheese is bubbling.

Ingredients

6 jalapeno peppers
1 batch Cheese Sauce
1 cup raw cashews
1/4–1/2 cup chopped red bell pepper
2 tablespoons olive oil
2 tablespoons water
1 1/2 tablespoons lemon juice
1/2 teaspoon sea salt
1 teaspoon onion powder
1/4 teaspoon turmeric

Main Dishes

Bean Sliders

Prep Time: 5–10 minutes
Wait Time: 10 minutes

Grain free, sugar free, gluten free, dairy free   *Serves: 2–4*

Once finished, you can layer with tomato, pickle, and a slice of onion, and drizzle some ranch dressing on top.

Directions

1. In a food processor, add oil and beans and pulse until a paste forms.
2. Add the rest of the ingredients, except for the sesame seeds.
3. Pulse until a formable paste is made.
4. Roll into bite-sized balls (imagine a golf ball) and press down to form discs.
5. Coat with sesame seeds.
6. Bake in the oven at 350°F for 5 minutes on each side.

Ingredients

2 cups beans, rinsed and drained
1 cup almond meal
1 teaspoon cumin
1 teaspoon sea salt
½ teaspoon pepper
1 egg
1 garlic clove
½ teaspoon oregano
¼ cup onion, finely chopped
2 tablespoon sesame seeds to coat

Broccoli and Cauliflower Bake

Prep Time: 20 minutes
Wait Time: 30 minutes

Grain free, sugar free, gluten free   *Serves: 4*

You can also make this dairy free by substituting nutritional yeast for the cheese.

Directions

1. Preheat oven to 425°F.
2. Toss broccoli and cauliflower in a large bowl with 1 tablespoon of oil until well coated.
3. Divide between 2 baking sheets and spread in an even layer.
4. Roast the vegetables for 20–25 min, stirring once and rotating the pans top to bottom about halfway through, until tender and beginning to brown.
5. Meanwhile, heat 1 tablespoon of oil in a large saucepan over medium heat.
6. Add onion and cook for 5–8 minutes, stirring frequently, until very soft and golden brown.
7. Add flour, salt, and pepper; cook, stirring, for 1 minute more.
8. Add milk and continue to stir, scraping up any browned bits.
9. Cook, stirring, until the sauce bubbles and thickens enough to coat the back of a spoon, about 4 minutes.
10. Remove from the heat.
11. When the vegetables are done, remove from the oven.
12. Preheat the broiler.
13. Transfer half the vegetables to a 2-quart broiler-safe baking dish.
14. Spread half the sauce over the vegetables.
15. Add the remaining vegetables and top with the remaining sauce.
16. Combine almond meal and the remaining 1 tablespoon oil in a small bowl (skip this step if you are topping with cheese).
17. Sprinkle the almond meal mixture (or cheese) over the veggies.
18. Place under the broiler and broil, watching closely, until the veggies are bubbling and beginning to brown on top (1 to 5 minutes, depending on your broiler).
19. Let stand for 10 minutes before serving.

Ingredients

1 broccoli crown, trimmed and cut into 1-inch florets (about 4 cups)
1/2 head cauliflower, trimmed and cut into 1-inch florets (about 4 cups)
2–3 tablespoons extra-virgin olive oil, divided
1 medium onion, thinly sliced
3 tablespoons coconut flour
3/4 teaspoon salt
1/4 teaspoon black pepper
2 1/2 cups organic, raw milk or almond milk
1 1/2 cups almond meal
1/2 cup shredded or crumbled organic cheese

Hearty Chili

Prep Time: 5–10 minutes
Wait Time: 30 minutes

Grain free, sugar free, gluten free, dairy free   *Serves: 2–4*

Directions

1. Brown the beef in a pot.
2. Add the onion, zucchini, and carrots until softened.
3. Add remaining ingredients.
4. Simmer for at least 30 minutes.

Ingredients

1 1/2 pound ground organic beef
1/2 cup chopped onion
1 cup chopped zucchini
1 cup chopped carrots
Ground garlic
4 cups pureed tomatoes
1 can kidney beans
3 tablespoons chili powder
2 tablespoons apple cider vinegar
Water to thin out if needed

Basic Grilled Salmon

Prep Time: 5–10 minutes
Wait Time: 15 minutes

Grain free, sugar free, gluten free, dairy free   *Serves: 2*

This can also be done in the oven at 400°F for 10–15 minutes.

Directions

1. Preheat oven to 350°F.
2. Place salmon on top of lemon slices on a piece of parchment paper.
3. Sprinkle with dill and top with butter.
4. Bake or grill for 15 min or until salmon is perfectly pink and easily flakes.

Ingredients

1 (6 ounce) salmon
2 teaspoons fresh dill
1 tablespoon butter or ghee
1/2 lemon, thinly sliced

Layered Hamburger Bake

Prep Time: 15 minutes
Wait Time: 20 minutes

Grain free, sugar free, gluten free   *Serves: 6*

Another of my daughter and husband's favorites. My husband's favorite meal was always lasagna, and this resembles that dish very closely.

Directions

1. Preheat oven 350°F.
2. Melt coconut oil in skillet.
3. Add mushrooms and cook until browned.
4. Add ground beef to skillet and brown.
5. Add tomato sauce, garlic, pepper, and sea salt to skillet; simmer.
6. Mix in separate bowl, cream cheese, and sour cream until smooth.
7. Stir in onions.
8. Scoop half of cooked spaghetti squash into a casserole dish.
9. Cover with half of cheese mixture and half of meat mixture.
10. Add the remaining spaghetti squash, cheese mixture, and meat mixture.
11. Bake in oven for 20 minutes.
12. Remove from oven and cool for 10 minutes.

Ingredients

2 tablespoons coconut oil
1 cup mushrooms, sliced
1 pound ground beef
2 cups tomato sauce
1 clove garlic
1 teaspoon sea salt
Dash of pepper
1/4 cup organic cream cheese, softened
1 cup organic sour cream
1/2 onion, chopped
1 spaghetti squash

Creamy Broccoli and Sun-Dried Tomato Skillet

Prep Time: 5–10 minutes
Wait Time: 20 minutes

Grain free, sugar free, gluten free

Serves: 2–4

Directions

1. To prepare on stovetop, heat oil in skillet over medium-high heat 1–3 minutes or until shimmering.
2. Add onion and garlic; cook 30–45 seconds or until fragrant.
3. Stir in pasta, broth, and wine; cook, uncovered, 14–16 minutes or until almost all liquid is absorbed and pasta is tender.
4. Remove skillet from heat.
5. Add tomatoes and broccoli.
6. Cover; let stand 5 minutes.
7. Add cheeses; mix well.

Ingredients

1 medium onion
2 garlic cloves, pressed
2 teaspoon olive oil or ghee
1 1/2 cups uncooked spelt or bean pasta or quinoa
3 cups vegetable or chicken broth or water
3/4 cup dry white wine such as Chardonnay
1 jar sun-dried tomatoes in oil, drained and patted dry
1 head broccoli florets
1/4 cup parmesan cheese
3/4 cup organic cream cheese

Sweet and Spicy Beef Stir Fry

(Dr. Tom Recipe)

Prep Time: 15 minutes
Wait Time: 20 minutes

Grain free, gluten free, dairy free   *Serves: 2–4*

Directions

1. Brown beef in a pan and set aside.
2. Sauté vegetables in coconut oil.
3. In a separate small pan, sauté garlic in coconut oil.
4. Add hot sauce and honey to garlic and mix well.
5. Toss beef and vegetables in sauce.

Ingredients

Coconut oil
1 pound grass-fed beef stir fry
1 bag/bunch frozen or fresh stir-fry vegetables
1/2 cup Frank's Red Hot Sauce
1/4 cup raw honey
2 cloves garlic, minced

Savory Beef Lettuce Wraps

Prep Time: 5–10 minutes
Wait Time: 20 minutes

Grain free, sugar free, gluten free, dairy free   *Serves: 4–6*

You can also stuff this into peppers.

Directions

1. Cook beef in skillet about 5 minutes, until beef crumbles and is no longer pink.
2. Add mushrooms and all ingredients except the green onions.
3. Cook on medium-high heat for 4 minutes, stirring constantly.
4. Add green onions (if desired) and cook 1 minute.
5. Spoon mixture evenly onto lettuce leaves; roll up.

Ingredients

1 pound ground beef
1 cup mushrooms, chopped
3 tablespoons almond/cashew butter
1 tablespoon sesame oil
1 tablespoon apple cider vinegar
1 cup zucchini, chopped
3 cloves garlic, minced
2 tablespoons fresh ginger, minced
1/3 cup tamari or coconut aminos
1/2 cup green onions, chopped (optional)
1 head lettuce, separated into leaves

Lettuce Wrap Tacos

(Dr. Tom Recipe)

Prep Time: 10 minutes
Wait Time: 20 minutes

Grain free, sugar free, gluten free, dairy free   *Serves: 2–4*

Perfect for Taco Tuesdays!

Directions

1. Brown ground beef in skillet.
2. Drain grease.
3. Add in all spices and water.
4. Bring to a boil, then reduce to simmer until mixture thickens.
5. Assemble beef in lettuce wrap or tortillas
6. Top with any of your favorite toppings.

Toppings: grass-fed cheese, avocado, diced red onion, organic sour cream (optional)

Ingredients

1 pound grass-fed ground beef
Bibb lettuce or romaine lettuce boats
1 tablespoon chili powder
1 tablespoon cumin
1/2 teaspoon garlic powder
1/2 teaspoon onion powder
2 teaspoons salt and pepper
2/3 cup water

Sundried Tomato Chicken Bake

(Dr. Tom Recipe)

Prep Time: 15 minutes
Wait Time: 30 minutes

Grain free, sugar free, gluten free   *Serves: 2–4*

We like any recipe that involves only one pan. For this one, we used a cast iron skillet. You will need to cook on the stovetop and then the oven, so the cast iron worked perfectly.

Directions

1. Preheat oven to 375°F.
2. Melt half the butter in a cast iron skillet (or oven-proof pan).
3. Add garlic and red pepper flakes and sauté 1–2 minutes.
4. Whisk in chicken broth, sun-dried tomatoes, parmesan, thyme, oregano, basil, coconut milk, and remaining butter.
5. Bring mixture to a boil, then reduce heat to a simmer until it thickens slightly.
6. Add chicken to pan and season with salt and pepper.
7. Place the whole skillet in the oven and cook for about 25–30 minutes until chicken is cooked through.
   Note: For a thicker sauce, you can use a separate pan to whisk coconut milk with melted butter and 2 tablespoons arrowroot powder, and then add this mixture to the skillet.

Ingredients

2 chicken breasts, organic
4 tablespoons grass-fed organic butter, divided
1 cup organic chicken broth
3 cloves garlic, minced
1/4 teaspoon red pepper flakes
1/3 cup sun-dried tomatoes, diced
1/2 cup coconut milk
1/4 cup parmesan cheese, organic
Thyme, oregano, basil, salt, pepper to taste

White Chicken Chili

(Dr. Tom Recipe)

Prep Time: 20 minutes
Wait Time: 7 hours

Grain free, sugar free, gluten free   *Serves: 2–4*

This is a great substitute when chicken soup just seems too boring—and it's made in the slow cooker, which is probably the best kitchen invention ever. Enjoy!

Directions

1. Place chicken, all spices, beans, celery, bell pepper, onion, and broth in slow cooker.
2. Cook on low for 6 hours.
3. With about one hour left to cook, use the coconut milk, butter, and arrowroot together as a mixture to thicken the chili. To do this, melt butter in pan. Whisk arrowroot into melted butter, then gradually whisk in the coconut milk.
4. Simmer this mixture for about 3–5 minutes until it is thickened.
5. Then add the mixture to the slow cooker and let the soup continue cooking.
6. At this point, you can also add the cream cheese to the slow cooker.
7. Before serving, make sure to shred the chicken in the slow cooker.
8. Put sliced avocado, diced green onion, and grated cheese on top of soup in bowl before serving.

Ingredients

3–4 organic chicken breasts (vary this based on number of servings)
1 can white beans, rinsed and drained
1 carton organic chicken broth (no sugar added)—ounces can range from 15–36 depending on amount of veggies/chicken
4 celery stalks, diced
1 organic white or yellow onion, chopped
1 green or red organic bell pepper, diced
1 bunch organic green onions, diced
Chili powder, onion powder, garlic powder, cumin, salt, and pepper to taste
1 avocado
1 cup grass-fed cheese. grated
1 cup coconut milk
3 tablespoons grass-fed butter
3 tablespoons arrowroot powder
1/2 package organic cream cheese (optional)

Buffalo Chicken Spaghetti Squash

(Dr. Tom Recipe)

Prep Time: 40 minutes
Wait Time: 30 minutes

Grain free, sugar free, gluten free   *Serves: 2–4*

Serve with homemade ranch dressing (see page 125).

Directions

1. Preheat oven to 425°F.
2. Chicken and spaghetti squash should be cooked first.
3. Sauté celery, onion, carrot, and garlic in coconut oil.
4. Stir in the cooked chicken to heat through.
5. Add coconut milk and hot sauce to the chicken and veggie mixture.
6. Stir to combine and then turn off the heat.
7. Stir in the cheese.
8. Add the spaghetti squash strands to the mixture and stir well.
9. Pour the entire mixture into a casserole dish and top with extra cheese, if desired.
10. Bake, covered, for 25 minutes.
11. Uncover and bake for 10 more minutes.
12. Let stand for 5 minutes before serving.

Ingredients

1/4 cup each of carrot, celery, and red onion, diced
2 cloves garlic, minced
1 medium spaghetti squash, roasted and deseeded
2–3 chicken breasts, cooked and shredded
1 cup coconut milk
1/4–1/2 cup hot sauce, to taste
1 cup organic shredded mozzarella cheese

Baked Cheesy Chicken Breast

Prep Time: 5–10 minutes
Wait Time: 30 minutes

Grain free, sugar free, gluten free   *Serves: 2–4*

Directions

1. Preheat oven at 375°F.
2. Mix mayonnaise, cheese, and seasonings.
3. Spread mixture over chicken breast and place in a baking dish.
4. Bake for 30 minutes.

Ingredients

4 boneless chicken breast halves
1 cup mayonnaise
1/2 cup grated parmesan cheese
1 1/2 teaspoons seasoning salt
1/2 teaspoon ground black pepper
1 teaspoon garlic powder
1/2 teaspoon cayenne powder

Chicken Breast Supreme

Prep Time: 25 minutes
Wait Time: 2 hours

Grain free, sugar free, gluten free

Serves: 5–6 (makes 8–10 breast halves)

Directions

1. Preheat oven at 325°F.
2. Put a single layer of prosciutto on the bottom of a buttered casserole dish.
3. Cut chicken breasts in half.
4. Put a strip of bacon around each breast and fasten with a toothpick.
5. Mix sour cream with cream of mushroom soup.
6. Spread over the top of chicken breasts.
7. Sprinkle paprika on top.
8. Bake for 2 hours or until tender.

Ingredients

5 chicken breasts
10 slices of beef bacon
1 cup organic sour cream
1 cup cream of mushroom soup
Sprinkle of paprika
8 slices of prosciutto or dried beef

Honey Mustard Chicken

Prep Time: 5–10 minutes
Wait Time: 20 minutes

Grain free, gluten free, dairy free   *Serves: 2–4*

This is a perfect recipe to use up leftover chicken.

Directions

1. Cut chicken breasts into strips (or dice it).
2. Cook on stove in a pan for 5 minutes per side or until cooked through.
3. While chicken is cooking, stir the rest of the ingredients together.
4. Once the chicken is ready, pour the honey mustard mix on top of the chicken.
5. Let simmer for 15 minutes.

Ingredients

2 chicken breasts
1/4 cup Dijon mustard
1/4 cup raw honey
Sea salt and pepper to taste

Sirloin Dijon

Prep Time: 15 minutes
Wait Time: 20 minutes

Grain free, sugar free, gluten free, dairy free   *Serves: 2–4*

Directions

1. Sauté the sirloin and garlic in coconut oil until sirloin starts to brown.
2. While the sirloin is browning, sprinkle with salt and pepper.
3. In a separate bowl, mix together the chicken stock, thyme, and mustard.
4. Pour the mustard mixture over the sirloin and bring to a simmer.
5. Add the kale to the pan and cook, stirring often until the kale is tender.

Ingredients

1 1/2 pounds sirloin, thinly sliced
3 garlic cloves, crushed
2 tablespoons coconut oil
Sea salt and black pepper to taste
1/2 cup chicken stock
1/2 tablespoon dried thyme
1/2 tablespoon mustard
4 cups kale or spinach, chopped

One-Pot Chicken Fajitas

Prep Time:15 minutes
Wait Time: 10 minutes

Grain free, sugar free, gluten free   *Serves: 2–4*

I love the recipes that only require one pot and about 15 minutes.

Directions

1. Heat 2 tablespoons of oil and chicken into a pot until cooked.
2. Remove chicken from the pot and add peppers and onions.
3. Sauté for 8 minutes or until soft.
4. Add chicken back to the pot and add all spices.
5. Stir until fragrant, then add liquids and pasta.
6. Cook until pasta is soft and ready, then add the cheese.
7. Stir to mix everything together and until the cheese is melted.
8. Serve hot!

Ingredients

3 chicken breast, diced or cut in slices
1 each: red, green, and yellow peppers, chopped
1 onion, chopped
1 tablespoon cumin
1 tablespoon chili powder
1 tablespoon garlic
1 teaspoon sea salt
1 teaspoon ground pepper
3 cups coconut milk
2 cups vegetable or chicken broth
4 cups red lentil penne pasta
1 cup organic shredded cheese

Chicken and Broccoli Stir Fry

Prep Time: 10 minutes
Wait Time: 20 minutes

Grain free, sugar free, gluten free, dairy free   *Serves: 2–4*

Directions

1. Heat 1 teaspoon of oil in a fry pan over medium heat.
2. Add the broccoli and mushrooms and cook for approximately 4 minutes or until vegetables are tender.
3. Add the ginger and garlic to the pan and cook for 30 seconds.
4. Remove the vegetables from the pan; place them on a plate and cover.
5. Wipe the pan clean with a paper towel and turn the heat to high.
6. Add the remaining tablespoon of oil.
7. Season the chicken pieces with salt and pepper
8. Add them to the pan in a single layer.
9. Cook for 3–4 minutes on each side until golden brown and cooked through.
10. Add the vegetables back to the pan and cook for 2 more minutes or until the vegetables are warmed through.
11. In a bowl, whisk together the oyster sauce, chicken broth, sesame oil and coconut aminos.
12. In a small bowl, mix the arrowroot powder with a tablespoon of cold water.
13. Pour the oyster sauce mixture over the chicken and vegetables.
14. Cook for 30 seconds.
15. Add the arrowroot powder and bring to a boil.
16. Cook for 1 more minute, or until sauce has just started to thicken.

Ingredients

1 pound boneless skinless chicken breast, cut into 1-inch pieces
4 teaspoons avocado or olive oil
2 cups small broccoli florets
1 cup mushrooms, sliced
2 teaspoons fresh ginger, minced
1 teaspoon garlic, minced
1/4 cup oyster sauce
1/4 cup organic or homemade chicken broth or water
2 teaspoons sesame oil
1 teaspoon coconut aminos
1 teaspoon arrowroot powder
salt and pepper to taste

Chicken and Sweet Potato Casserole

(Dr. Tom Recipe)

Prep Time: 15–20 minutes
Wait Time: 60 minutes

Grain free, sugar free, gluten free   *Serves: 2–4*

Directions

1. Preheat oven to 400°F.
2. Prepare a 9" × 13" baking dish with cooking spray.
3. In a large bowl, mix together the olive oil, salt, pepper, paprika, garlic powder, and hot sauce.
4. Add the sweet potatoes and chicken and stir to coat.
5. Carefully scoop the sweet potatoes and chicken into the prepared baking dish.
6. Bake the sweet potatoes and chicken for 55–60 minutes, stirring every 20 minutes, until cooked through, crispy, and browned on the outside.
7. While the potatoes are cooking, fry the bacon (about half a pound).
8. Once the potatoes and chicken are fully cooked, remove them from the oven.
9. Top the cooked potatoes with the cheese, bacon, and green onion.
10. Return the casserole to the oven.
11. Bake for 5 minutes or until cheese is melted.

Ingredients

1 pound boneless chicken breasts, cubed
6–8 medium sweet potatoes, peeled and cubed
1/3 cup olive oil
1 teaspoon salt
1/2 teaspoon black pepper
1 tablespoon paprika
2 tablespoons garlic powder
2 tablespoons hot sauce
2 cups organic cheese, shredded
1 cup crumbled organic beef or turkey bacon, no sugar added
1 cup green onion, diced

Roast with Balsamic and Dijon

Prep Time: 30 minutes
Wait Time: 3 hours

Grain free, sugar free, gluten free, dairy free   *Serves: 4–6*

Directions

1. Preheat oven to 300°F.
2. Heat oil in a large Dutch oven over high heat.
3. Season chuck roast well with salt and pepper, add to a pan, and brown well on all sides (a few minutes per side).
4. Remove roast and set aside.
5. Add chopped onion to drippings in pot and reduce heat to medium.
6. Sauté onions until soft, about 5 minutes.
7. Add balsamic vinegar and increase heat to medium-high.
8. Boil until reduced and slightly syrupy, about 4–5 more minutes.
9. Stir in Dijon mustard.
10. Set roast on top of onions in pot.
11. Pour in beef broth and add thyme.
12. Cover and place in oven for 2 1/2–3 hours or until very tender.
13. Add carrots and potatoes to pot and return to oven.
14. Continue cooking until carrots and potatoes are tender, 30–60 minutes.

Ingredients

2–3 tablespoons olive oil
4 pounds chuck roast
1 medium to large onion, chopped
1/3 cup balsamic vinegar
2–3 tablespoons Dijon mustard
1–2 tablespoon dried thyme
2 cups beef broth or water
2 medium carrots, chopped
1 medium sweet potato, chopped
Sea salt and freshly ground black pepper

Stuffed Acorn Squash Goodness

Prep Time: 20 minutes
Wait Time: 50 minutes

Grain free, sugar free, gluten free   *Serves: 2–4*

Directions

1. Preheat oven 400°F.
2. Drizzle olive oil, sea salt, and pepper in squash.
3. Roast for 20 minutes or until soft to pierce with a fork.
4. While the squash is cooking, heat oil in skillet.
5. Add veggies and sauté for 6–8 minutes.
6. Add ground beef and cook until no longer pink.
7. Add spices, flour, and cheese.
8. Simmer for 8 minutes.
9. Once squash is done, fill it with the filling and bake for 20 minutes.
10. Remove from oven and cool for 5 minutes.

Ingredients

1 acorn squash, halved and deseeded
2 celery stalks, chopped
1/2 onion, chopped
1/2 cup mushrooms, chopped
1/2 pound ground beef
2 garlic cloves, minced
2 tablespoons coconut oil
1/2 cup almond flour
1/4 cup organic parmesan cheese (optional)
Sea salt
Pepper
Nutmeg

Zucchini Beef Skillet

Prep Time: 5 – 10 minutes
Wait Time: 20 minutes

Grain free, sugar free, gluten free, dairy free   *Serves: 2 – 4*

Directions

1. Cook beef, onion, and green pepper in a large skillet until slightly browned.
2. Add other ingredients.
3. Cover and simmer until tender.
4. Sprinkle with fresh parmesan cheese (optional).

Ingredients

1 pound grass-fed ground beef
1 cup chopped onion
3/4 cup green pepper, chopped
1/2 teaspoon sea salt
1/4 teaspoon pepper
1 teaspoon chili powder
4 or 5 cups sliced zucchini
2 large tomatoes, peeled and chopped

Shepherd's Pie

Prep Time: 15 minutes
Wait Time: 50 minutes

Grain free, sugar free, gluten free, dairy free   *Serves: 2–4*

Another dish inspired by my travels. I loved the meat pies in London!

Directions

1. Preheat oven to 375°F.
2. Boil potatoes in water and simmer until they are soft. Once soft, mash in a bowl and set aside.
3. Line a greased baking dish with sweet potatoes.
4. Mix remaining ingredients and pour into the baking dish.
5. Cover with the remainder of sweet potatoes.
6. Bake for 45 minutes.
7. Brush surface with coconut milk to brown.
8. Broil for 2–3 minutes.

Ingredients

4 cups sweet potatoes, chopped
3 cups ground beef, browned
1/4 cup onion, chopped
3/4 cup carrots, cooked
3/4 cup green beans, steamed
1/2 cup almond meal
1/2 cup coconut milk
1 egg, beaten
1 teaspoon sea salt
Pepper to taste

Zucchini Layered Lasagna

Prep Time: 20 minutes
Wait Time: 45 minutes

Grain free, sugar free, gluten free

Serves: 4–6

Directions

1. Preheat oven to 350°F.
2. Brown meat in a skillet until no longer pink.
3. Drain the excess fat and add tomatoes, tomato paste, oregano, and garlic salt.
4. Line zucchini noodles on bottom of baking pan.
5. Set aside 1 cup of the meat sauce.
6. Place half of meat sauce on top of zucchini and ½ of cheese mix on top of meat sauce.
7. Layer again in the same order.
8. Sprinkle the cup of reserved meat sauce on top and sprinkle mozzarella cheese on top.
9. Bake for 45 minutes.
10. Let cool for 15 minutes.

Ingredients

1 pound ground beef or turkey
3 1/2 cups crushed tomatoes
1 1/2 cup tomato paste
1 1/2 teaspoon oregano
1–2 teaspoon garlic salt
1/3 cup parmesan cheese
2 cup full fat cottage cheese
2 cup mozzarella cheese, shredded
1–2 zucchinis, sliced lengthwise in the shape of a lasagna noodle

Sneaky Meatballs

Prep Time: 15 minutes
Wait Time: 25 minutes

Grain free, sugar free, gluten free, dairy free   *Serves: 6*

This is a family favorite and I mean the whole family, children included. I usually double batch this recipe and freeze to have on days where there wasn't a lot of time in the kitchen.

Directions

1. Preheat oven to 425°F.
2. In a food processor, add all vegetables and pulse until finely chopped.
3. Place ground beef in a deep mixing bowl and add the chopped vegetables to it, along with all other ingredients.
4. Form golf-sized balls and place on a parchment-lined cookie sheet.
5. Cook for 20–25 minutes or until no longer pink in the middle.

Ingredients

1 pound grass-fed ground beef
1 zucchini, peeled
1 carrot or 1/2 sweet potato
1/2 red onion
1 garlic clove
2 eggs
1/2 cup almond flour
1 teaspoon each: oregano, cumin, and sea salt
Ground pepper to taste

Simple Baked Fish

Prep Time: 15 minutes
Wait Time: 20 minutes

Grain free, sugar free, gluten free, dairy free   *Serves: 2–4*

Directions

1. Preheat oven to 325°F.
2. Pat fish dry.
3. Mix mayonnaise and mustard in a bowl.
4. Combine the rest of the ingredients on a separate plate.
5. Coat fish with mustard and mayo mixture.
6. Roll in dry ingredients.
7. Place on a parchment-lined cookie sheet
8. Bake until flaky, usually around 15–20 minutes.

Ingredients

1 pound white fish of your choice
1/4 cup homemade mayonnaise
1/4 cup yellow or Dijon mustard
1/2 cup almond flour
1/4 cup shredded coconut
1 teaspoon sea salt
A dash cayenne pepper

Desserts

Puppy Chow
Page 108

"Sugared" Mix Nut Medley
Page 109

Mom's Butter Pecan Bars
Page 110

Almond Flour Cookies

Prep Time: 10 minutes
Wait Time: 10 minutes

Grain free, sugar free, gluten free, dairy free   *Serves: 4–6*

These cookies are very basic and versatile. You can use them to make the fruit pizza, or you can add some chocolate chips or shredded coconut.

Directions

1. Preheat oven to 350°F.
2. Mix all ingredients.
3. Let chill in the refrigerator for 30 minutes.
4. Roll out onto a flat surface sprinkled with coconut flour.
5. You can use a cookie cutter or just roll the dough into balls and flatten them.
6. Bake for 8–10 minutes.

Ingredients

1 cup almond flour
1 egg
1 tablespoon coconut oil
1 teaspoon vanilla or almond extract
Stevia to taste

Flax Chocolate Chip Cookies

Prep Time: 40 minutes
Wait Time: 15 minutes

Grain free, sugar free, gluten free

Serves: 6–8 (makes about 25 cookies)

These cookies definitely hit the sweet spot, and toddlers love them. These make great ice cream sandwiches, too.

Directions

1. Preheat oven to 350°F. Line a cookie sheet with parchment paper.
2. In a large bowl, mix flour, flax, chocolate chips, cacao powder, baking soda, and salt.
3. Add egg and vanilla to the flour, but do not mix yet.
4. On the stovetop, melt the butter and honey in a pot.
5. Remove the melted mixture from the heat. Add coconut sugar and allow it to dissolve.
6. Add melted butter mixture to the dry ingredients and mix well.
7. Cover dough and chill in refrigerator for 30 minutes.
8. Line cookie sheet with parchment paper and spread coconut oil.
9. Measure about one tablespoon of dough and flatten.
10. Place on cookie sheet about an inch apart and bake for 12 minutes.
11. Remove from oven and cool for 5 minutes.

Ingredients

1 1/3 cups buckwheat flour, sifted
1/3 cup milled flax
1/3 cup sugar-free chocolate chips
1 tablespoon raw cacao powder
1 1/2 teaspoon baking soda
1/2 teaspoon salt
1/2 cup butter or ghee
1/4 cup coconut sugar
1/4 cup raw honey
1 1/2 teaspoon vanilla
1 egg

Vanilla Coconut Milk Ice Cream

Prep Time: 10 minutes
Wait Time: 30 minutes

Grain free, gluten free, dairy free   *Serves: 2-4*

Directions

1. Blend all ingredients in a blender.
2. Pour the blended mixture into an ice cream maker and follow the manufacturer's directions.

Ingredients

3-3 1/2 cups coconut milk
1/2 cup raw honey
2 tablespoon vanilla
1/2 scoop vanilla protein

Chocolate Cashew Butter Ice Cream

Prep Time: 10 minutes
Wait Time: 30 minutes

Grain free, gluten free, dairy free   *Serves: 2-4*

This is always a favorite of ours, and we make it often during the summer months. If you will be serving this later, remove the ice cream from the freezer 30 minutes before serving, because it can take a while to thaw enough to scoop.

Directions

1. Mix all ingredients in blender.
2. Pour the blended mixture into an ice cream maker and follow the manufacturer's directions.

Ingredients

3 cups coconut milk
1 cup cashew butter
1/2 cup cocoa powder
1/4 cup raw honey or pure maple syrup
2 teaspoons vanilla extract

Strawberry Gelato

Prep Time: 10 minutes
Wait Time: 30 minutes

Grain free, sugar free, gluten free, dairy free   *Serves: 2–4*

This recipe was inspired by my trip to France. I was so impressed with the pure ingredients and the taste of French gelato that I had to make sure to include my own take on it in this book. The avocado gives it that creamy texture without any need for milk.

Directions

1. Put the strawberries and avocado in a high-powered blender (preferably one with a plunger).
2. Blend well, then add stevia to taste. It won't take much, because the strawberries are sweet on their own.
3. Pour the blended mixture into an ice cream maker and follow the manufacturer's directions.

Ingredients

1 1/2 cup frozen strawberries
1/2 scoop vanilla protein powder
1 ripe avocado, pit and peel removed
Stevia to taste

Lemon Poppyseed Muffins

Prep Time: 10 minutes
Wait Time: 30 minutes

Grain free, gluten free, dairy free   *Serves: 6*

I made these for my youngest's first birthday party, but instead of adding poppyseeds, I added a few blueberries and iced them with a coconut cream icing.

Directions

1. Preheat oven to 350°F.
2. Combine coconut flour, salt, and baking soda in a smaller bowl.
3. In a larger bowl, blend eggs, honey, avocado oil, and lemon zest.
4. Mix dry into wet.
5. Fold in poppy seeds.
6. Spoon 1 tablespoon of batter into greased mini muffin tins. (Or, if using paper muffin cups, grease inside the of each cup with a little oil to prevent the muffins from sticking to the paper.)
7. Bake for 15 minutes.

Ingredients

6 tablespoons coconut flour
1/2 teaspoon salt
1/4 teaspoon baking soda
3 eggs
1/8 cup raw honey or maple syrup
1/4 cup avocado oil
1 tablespoon lemon zest
1 tablespoon poppy seeds

Fruit Pizza

Prep Time: 15 minutes
Wait Time: 10 minutes

Grain free, gluten free

Serves: 2–4

Directions

1. Preheat oven to 350°F.
2. Let cookie dough soften at room temperature.
3. Pat thinly onto a large cookie sheet.
4. Bake for 10 minutes.
5. Mix the cream cheese, honey, and coconut milk until light and fluffy.
6. Spread over cooked cookie crust.
7. Mix fruits together and spread over cream cheese layer. Extra fruit may be added to taste.
8. Slice squares and serve chilled.

If you want a glaze in between the cream cheese and fruit layers, you can simmer 1 cup of raspberries over low heat, blend to a smooth texture, and drizzle it onto the cream cheese layer.

Ingredients

1 batch of almond flour cookie dough
1 cup organic cream cheese
3/4 cup honey
1 cup coconut milk, chilled
2 bananas, sliced
1 cup strawberries, sliced
1/2 cup pineapple, sliced
1 kiwi, peeled and sliced

Warm Apple Crisp

Prep Time: 15 minutes
Wait Time: 30 minutes

Grain free, sugar free, gluten free   *Serves: 2–4*

Directions

1. Preheat oven to 375°F.
2. Core and slice apples.
3. Arrange apples in a greased baking dish with 5 tablespoons of softened butter randomly dispersed overtop.
4. Cover and bake until apples start to soften, around 10–15 minutes.
5. In a separate bowl, sift dry ingredients together.
6. Add melted butter and vanilla extract to the dry ingredients.
7. Thoroughly mix together, then crumble over apples.
8. Place back in the oven.
9. Bake uncovered until topping starts to brown and "crisp," close to 20 minutes.
10. Top with whipped coconut cream or homemade ice cream as desired.

Ingredients

5 large granny smith apples
1 cup almond flour
1/4 cup hemp heart seeds
2 tablespoons of milled flaxseed
2 teaspoons cinnamon
1 teaspoon nutmeg
1/2 teaspoon vanilla extract
4–5 teaspoons stevia
8 tablespoons butter or ghee (5 softened, 3 melted)

Chocolate Cupcakes

Prep Time: 15 minutes
Wait Time: 25 minutes

Grain free, sugar free, gluten free, dairy free   *Serves: 6–8*

My favorite topping for these cupcakes is the Cashew Butter Frosting!

Directions

1. Preheat oven to 325°F.
2. Line cupcake pan with parchment paper and grease with coconut oil.
3. Drain and rinse beans in a strainer or colander.
4. Shake off excess water.
5. Crack three of the eggs into the blender and add beans, vanilla, and salt.
6. Blend on high until beans are completely smooth.
7. Whisk together cocoa powder, baking soda, and baking powder.
8. Beat butter with coconut sugar until light and fluffy.
9. Add remaining two eggs, beating for a minute after each addition.
10. Pour bean batter into egg mixture and mix.
11. Finally, stir in cocoa powder.
12. Beat the batter on high for one minute until smooth.
13. Pour batter into each cupcake liners (about ¼ cup each).
14. Bake for 20–25 minutes or until cooked through.
15. Cupcakes are done when the tops are rounded and firm to the touch.
16. After 10 minutes, turn cupcake pan over onto a cooling rack. Let cool until cupcakes reach room temperature.

Ingredients

1 1/2 cups cooked black beans
5 large eggs, divided
1 tablespoon pure vanilla extract
1/2 teaspoon sea salt
6 tablespoons unsalted organic butter or coconut oil
1 cup coconut sugar
6 tablespoons unsweetened cocoa powder
1 teaspoon aluminum-free baking powder
1/2 teaspoon baking soda

Cashew Butter Frosting

Prep Time: 5 minutes
Wait Time: 15 minutes

Grain free, gluten free, dairy free   *Serves: 2–4*

Use this frosting right away. Once you put it in the refrigerator, it will harden.

Directions

1. Chill a can of coconut milk in the refrigerator overnight.
2. In the morning, turn the can upside down and scoop out the cream.
3. Using a mixer, beat the cream until it is light and fluffy.
4. Add the cashew butter 1 tablespoon at a time.
5. Add in the sweetener 1 tablespoon at a time.

Ingredients

1/2 can coconut cream
4 tablespoons raw cashew butter
2 tablespoons pure maple syrup or stevia to taste

Rich Chocolate Covered Nut Butter Rounds

Prep Time: 15–20 minutes
Wait Time: 60 minute

Grain free, gluten free   *Serves: 2–4*

This is so perfectly rich and packed with protein. These can be "naked" or chocolate-covered. If choosing to do the "naked" version, I recommend throwing some cocoa nibs or raisins in.

Directions

1. Melt the butter and cashew butter together.
2. Whisk in the cream cheese until well blended and smooth.
3. Add the sweetener and whey protein powder and blend well.
4. Line an 8" x 8" baking dish with parchment paper and spread the mixture in the dish.
5. Chill for about 30 minutes.
6. Roll into balls, about 1 tablespoon in size.
7. Freeze for an hour.

For the chocolate
1. Melt coconut oil over a very low heat in a double boiler.
2. Stir in cocoa, sweetener, and vanilla.
3. Dip the balls into the chocolate. You can use a toothpick and insert it into the ball while you are covering it in chocolate.
4. Lay the dipped rounds on a parchment-lined cookie sheet.
5. Place in freezer until chocolate is frozen.

Ingredients

1/2 cup butter or ghee, organic
1/2 cup raw cashew butter
4 ounces cream cheese
1/2 cup raw honey or 5–8 tablespoon pure stevia
1/3 cup chocolate Nature Pro Protein powder

For the chocolate
1 cup coconut oil
1 cup cocoa or carob powder
2 teaspoons vanilla
Stevia to taste (this can vary depending on how sweet you want it)

Surprise Chocolate Mousse

Prep Time: 15–20 minutes
Wait Time: 2 hours

Grain free, gluten free   *Serves: 4–6*

Directions

1. Melt chocolate chips in a double boiler, stirring often.
2. In a blender, combine avocados, melted chocolate, maple syrup, cocoa, milk, vanilla, and salt.
3. Cover and blend until smooth.
4. Dish into small serving bowls.
5. Refrigerate for 2 hours before serving.
6. Serve with raspberries.

Ingredients

1/3 cup chocolate chips, no sweetener
4 ripe avocados
2/3 cup maple syrup
1/3 cup unsweetened cocoa powder
1/4 cup almond milk or coconut milk
2 teaspoons vanilla extract
Pinch of sea salt
1/2 cup raspberries

Puppy Chow

Prep Time: 10 minutes
Wait Time: 30 minutes

Grain free, gluten free, dairy free   *Serves: 6–8*

Directions

1. Melt the chocolate chips over a double boiler on the stove.
2. Once the chocolate is melted, stir in the coconut oil and honey.
3. Once incorporated, stir in the nut butter until smooth, then stir in the nuts and coat well.
4. Throw the mixture into a large bowl with a lid.
5. Add the arrowroot powder.
6. Secure the lid on the container and then shake vigorously to coat the nuts.

Ingredients

1/2 cup dark chocolate chips, no sugar added
1/4 cup nut butter (cashew, almond, sun butter)
1 cup sliced almonds
1/2 cup pecans
1/2 cup walnuts
1/3 cup raw honey
1/4 cup coconut oil
4–6 tablespoons arrowroot powder

"Sugared" Mixed Nut Medley

Prep Time: 15 minutes
Wait Time: 30 minutes

Grain free, gluten free, dairy free   *Serves: 4–6*

These are great for party snacks or holidays.

Directions

1. Preheat oven to 300°F.
2. Dissolve sugar in water over medium heat.
3. Add mixed nuts and cook, stirring often until nuts are sugared and all syrup is used.
4. Pour on ungreased cookie sheet.
5. Bake for 30 minutes.
6. Stir 3–4 times while baking.
7. Store in an airtight container.

Ingredients

1/2 cup coconut sugar
1/4 cup raw honey
1/2 cup water
2 cups raw nuts (cashews, pecans, walnuts, almonds)

Mom's Butter Pecan Bars

Prep Time: 10 minutes
Wait Time: 35 minutes

Dairy free

Serves: 6–8

I recommend not making these all the time and limiting how many you are eating, but they are great to have every once in a while, or for special occasions.

Directions

1. Preheat oven to 350°F.
2. Beat the eggs in a bowl.
3. Add the sugar and honey.
4. Add the remaining ingredients and mix well.
5. Pour into greased and floured 9 x 13 pan.
6. Bake for 30–35 minutes.
7. Once cooled, cut into bars. These will be "hard" and crumbly.

Ingredients

2 eggs
1 cup coconut sugar
1 cup raw honey
3/4 cup melted butter
1 1/4 cup sifted spelt flour or buckwheat flour
1 cup chopped pecans
1 teaspoon vanilla

Homemade Staples

Soft Tortilla Wraps

Prep Time:20 minutes
Wait Time: 10 minutes

Sugar free, dairy free

Serves: 6–8 (makes about 10–12 wraps)

For those who are trying to stay gluten free, I have done these with cassava or buckwheat flour, but it is a little stickier, and the wraps come out crispier. I usually double the batch and store 14 in the freezer. Just make sure you put parchment paper in between the wraps if you are freezing them.

Directions

1. Put flour and sea salt in a tall mixing bowl and slowly add olive oil, incorporating with a fork.
2. Slowly add water. You may have to mix the water at the end with your hands.
3. Cover with a towel and set aside for 20 minutes.
4. Sprinkle flour on a surface and take about a golf size ball amount of dough and roll out on the surface.
5. You want to have the wrap rolled thin and as much in a circle as possible.
6. Heat a skillet with coconut oil until hot and place the tortilla on it.
7. Cook long enough so that it starts to bubble and flip.
8. Store in the refrigerator.

Ingredients

2 1/2 cups spelt flour
1/2 cup cold-pressed olive oil
1 cup warm water
Sea salt to taste
1 tablespoon coconut oil

Almond Pie Crust

Prep Time: 15 minutes
Wait Time: 10 minutes

Grain free, sugar free, gluten free   *Serves: 4–6*

Directions

1. Heat oven to 350°F.
2. Mix melted butter with almond meal and stevia.
3. Pat into a glass pie plate with your fingertips.
4. Gently heat in the oven for about 8 minutes.
5. Do not let the crust go brown.
6. Remove from oven and cool.

Ingredients

1 1/2 cups of almond meal or almond flour
1–2 teaspoons stevia
3 tablespoons of melted butter or ghee

Almond Milk

Prep Time: 10 minutes

Grain free, sugar free, gluten free, dairy free   *Serves: 6–8*

We are generally a dairy-free house, so this is very much a staple. If you read ingredients in store-bought almond milk, you will notice there are a lot of additives. When it is super easy to make, why not make it yourself?

Directions

1. Soak almonds for 8 hours.
2. Drain and rinse.
3. Place all ingredients in a blender.
4. Blend until smooth.
5. Strain in a nut milk bag over a bowl.
6. Squeeze bag until all liquid is out.
7. Store the milk in a glass jar in the fridge.

Keeps for about 2 weeks.

Keep the leftover pulp in a container in the refrigerator. I usually dehydrate my pulp at the end of the week and give it a few seconds in the blender to make it more fine, and voila! You have almond meal to make cookies with.

Ingredients

1 cup soaked almonds
5–6 cups filtered water
1–2 teaspoons vanilla
3 dates (optional)

Coconut Milk

Prep Time: 10 minutes

Grain free, sugar free, gluten free, dairy free   *Serves: 4–6*

I generally use more coconut milk because of all the nut allergies in schools, so this milk is perfect. I found that it actually tastes like coconut, which is quite different than store-bought coconut milk.

Directions

1. Add the ingredients to a high-speed blender.
2. Start at a low speed and increase speed to high for 3 minutes.
3. After 3 minutes, pour into a nut milk bag or cheesecloth with a bowl under the cloth.
4. Squeeze excess liquid out and pour liquid into a jar.
5. Store in the fridge for 5–7 days.

Just like the almond milk, you can keep the leftover pulp to dry and make coconut flour. This is very cost-effective because you are using the whole ingredient.

Ingredients

1 cup shredded coconut, unsweetened
2 cups hot water
*optional: 1/2 teaspoon vanilla

Horseradish Sauce

(Dr. Tom Recipe)

Prep Time: 10 minutes
Wait Time: 2 hours

Grain free, sugar free, gluten free   *Serves: 6–8*

This recipe is so quick and easy! We made it as a sauce to use on our grass-fed roast. The roast had its own juices, but the horseradish sauce added a ton of flavor! It will last in the fridge for at least a week.

Directions

1. Whisk all ingredients in a bowl.
2. Refrigerate for at least 2 hours.
3. Serve with your favorite roast!

Ingredients

1 cup grass-fed whole milk yogurt
1/4 cup grated horseradish
1 tablespoon Dijon mustard
1 teaspoon apple cider vinegar
1/2 teaspoon salt
1/4 teaspoon black pepper

Homemade Mayonnaise

Prep Time: 10 minutes

Grain free, sugar free, gluten free   *Serves: 4–6*

This is the easiest and best mayonnaise I've been able to come up with. The key is for everything to be at room temperature. It should have a very thick consistency.

Directions

1. In a high-speed blender or using an immersion blender, combine the eggs, mustard, salt, and 1/2 cup of oil.
2. Blend together for 20 seconds.
3. Slowly add the rest of the oil in a steady stream. It should become harder to mix because of the thickness.
4. At this point, you can add the lemon juice. You may need to stir with a spoon to mix the lemon juice in and finish up with a 20-second blend.

Ingredients

2 1/2 cups avocado oil
1 lemon, juiced and room temperature
2 teaspoons yellow mustard
1 teaspoon sea salt
2 eggs, room temperature

Homemade Ketchup

Prep Time: 5 minutes
Wait Time: 30 minutes

Grain free, sugar free, gluten free, dairy free   *Serves: 4–6*

My husband and daughter are obsessed with ketchup. It took a lot of trial and error to find one that they liked. I couldn't believe how every single ketchup out there has sugar in it!

Directions

1. Put all ingredients in a blender and blend until smooth.
2. Pour into a pot to simmer for about 30 minutes.
3. Store in an airtight container.

Lasts 10–14 days.

Ingredients

3/4 cup tomato paste
10 pitted Medjool dates
3/4 cup water
1/2 cup apple cider vinegar
1/2 lemon, juiced
1/2 teaspoon sea salt
1/2 teaspoon garlic powder
1/2 teaspoon onion powder

Chia Berry Jam

Prep Time: 15 minutes
Wait Time: 30 minutes

Grain free, gluten free, dairy free

Serves: 4–6

Directions

1. In a medium-sized saucepan, heat all ingredients except for the vanilla and chia seeds on medium heat.
2. Bring to a boil, then simmer for 20 minutes.
3. Remove from heat and add vanilla and chia seeds.
4. Mash the berries with a fork until they are well mashed.
5. Stir well and store in a jar. Place in the refrigerator for a few hours before serving.

Ingredients

3 cups berries (can be any berry)
2 tablespoons raw honey
3 tablespoons chia seeds
Splash of vanilla

Ranch Dressing/Dip

Prep Time: 10 minutes

Grain free, sugar free, gluten free   *Serves: 6–8*

This dip helps my toddler eat lots and lots of raw cauliflower and broccoli. She often chooses this as an afternoon snack over anything else. It's also a favorite of my husband's—he puts this on everything.

Directions

1. Whisk all ingredients together in bowl.
2. Store in a glass container in the refrigerator.

Keeps for 7 days.

Ingredients

1 cup grass-fed plain yogurt or homemade mayonnaise

1/4 cup coconut cream, if using mayonnaise

1 teaspoon each garlic powder, onion powder, and black pepper

1/2 teaspoon dill

1/2 tablespoon parsley

2 tablespoons apple cider vinegar

Chicken Bone Broth

Prep Time: 10 minutes
Wait Time: 8–10 hours

Grain free, sugar free, gluten free   *Serves: 6–8*

Broth was one of the first foods I gave my babies because it offers rich minerals and iron. I would mix a teaspoon in foods, which gives the food even more flavor.

Directions

1. Roughly chop all vegetables.
2. Add all ingredients to a slow cooker.
3. Cook on low for at least 9 hours. The longer you can let it cook, the better.
4. Strain liquid into a big bowl and use as you wish! I store mine in glass containers. If I have a surplus, I will freeze it in ice trays.

Ingredients

2 whole, organic, free-range chicken carcasses
2–3 whole carrots
2–3 celery stalks
1 white or yellow onion
3–4 cloves of garlic, smashed
2 tablespoons apple cider vinegar
Salt and pepper, to taste
Grated fresh ginger (optional)

Dr. Tom's Famous Party Salsa

Prep Time: 10 minutes

Grain free, sugar free, gluten free, dairy free   *Serves: 6–8*

Directions

1. Mix all ingredients gently in a bowl.
2. Add balsamic vinegar, olive oil, and salt and pepper to taste.
3. Do not add too much oil or vinegar, as the mixture will get soggy.
4. Serve with celery sticks, almond crackers, etc.

Ingredients

1 avocado, diced
1 tomato, diced
1/2 of a red onion, diced
1/2 cup goat cheese
Balsamic vinegar
Olive oil
Salt and pepper

Ghee or Clarified Butter

Prep Time: 5 minutes
Wait Time: 15–20 minutes

Grain free, sugar free, gluten free   *Serves: 6–8*

Directions

1. Melt butter in a saucepan over medium-low heat.
2. Stir occasionally.
3. Once all the butter is melted and there is a slightly brownish layer on the bottom of the pot, skim the white whey off the top and discard it.
4. Take remaining melted "butter" and pour it into a glass jar.
5. Let the ghee cool and somewhat solidify before putting it into the refrigerator.

Ingredients

1 pound of organic butter

Breastfeeding

The general recommendation is to breastfeed your babies exclusively until they are six months old, if possible. While this isn't possible for everybody, I like to have it as a primary goal because of the immunity it offers and the bond it can create between baby and mother. In my experience, drinking very large amounts of water and getting enough sleep were both very beneficial for my milk production. If formula needs to be introduced, it is always my recommendation that you spend a lot of time researching the type that you will use and find something with the most natural ingredients and lowest possible processed sugar content.

Feeding Babies

In my clinic, I work with many families. I cannot count how many times a week moms ask me, "What do you feed your children?" or "How do you get your toddler to eat vegetables?" I am not saying that it is super easy and every day is the same, but for the most part, both of my girls eat a very vegetable-heavy diet, and they have since we first introduced them to solid foods.

Our rule when we were first introducing solids was to only feed our daughters vegetables, and try to introduce as many as possible before their first birthday. On my oldest daughter's first birthday, she tried her first sweet food: blueberries. She had her first banana when she was almost two. The logic behind our food introduction schedule was that it would be harder to convince a child to eat vegetables once their palate was used to eating things that were sweet. Of course, some vegetables are a little sweeter, like sweet potatoes and carrots, but they are still vegetables. I'm going to share my experience and outline the plan that we followed. For the first year, I steamed most of the vegetables, and there were only a few baked items. I ended up making all the baby food because store-bought baby food typically contained something sweet, like mangos or bananas.

Once they had teeth, I felt comfortable not puréeing their food and let them work on

their hand-eye coordination and fine motor skills by picking up their own food. Admittedly, this method is always messier, but it is worth it to know that you are letting your child develop. You will also notice that I did not even think about adding any grains until 2 years old (or until her molars came in). A child's digestive enzymes are not fully developed until this time, so to feed her grains before that did not follow our plan. Even to this day, our youngest only eats grains on occasion— maybe every 2–3 weeks.

Below is an outline or example of what my schedule looked like when feeding our children. We eat the below foods often ourselves, so each time I made it for our family, I would fill several small containers for the children to eat over the next few days.

Our Baby Food Introduction Schedule

6 – 9 Months	Organic grass-fed beef bone broth, avocado, peas, green beans, zucchini, celery, mushrooms, squash, 1/3 tsp flaxseed and avocado oil
9 – 12 Months	Carrots, sweet potatoes, kale, spinach, cauliflower, broccoli, cabbage, brussel sprouts, asparagus, turnips, chicken, beef, turkey, egg yolk, cocnut/almond flour (I would make sweet potato "pancakes" and use coconut flour), almonds, pecans, walnuts (nuts/seeds used in baking only, not raw)
12 – 18 Months	Strawberries (my husband had an allergy when he was younger so I waited until closer to 18 months to introduce these), more herbs and spices, fish, beans, lentils, sea salt, honey/ maple syrup (in her birthday cake only)
2 Years +	Ancient grains, honey/maple syrup (in baking), bananas, oranges, grapes, pineapple

Feeding Toddlers and Older Kids:

I often get asked by frustrated parents of toddlers what I feed my children. Some parents feel they are negotiating or arguing with their children to eat healthy foods. Some have tried bribing their kids, and others have even resorted to making separate meals for separate people in their family. I tell everyone that my children eat exactly what the rest of the family eats. I cannot justify making several different meals, and I feel it better prepares them to become healthy adults.

Below, I have a few snack options that I send to school or have pre-made in the house. If you have children, you know how fast their metabolisms are; sometimes they need a caloric snack.

I regularly make a couple batches of ranch dressing that they can dip veggies in, and I love having an easily accessible basket in the refrigerator full of appropriate snacks.

Some different options I always have available in small containers are as follows:

Hard-boiled eggs	Applesauce cups/pouches
Bowl of grapes	Veggies and dip
Muffins	Fruit roll ups
Jello	Sliced apples
Water	100% juice

My daughter is very much a creature of habit. Her lunches are generally the same, which makes prep easier for us. An example of her ideal lunch is:

Spinach with homemade ranch dressing (this hardly ever changes)
½ avocado or handful of sweet potato fries
Slice of deli meat (no sulphites, no sugar, no additives) or other protein source
Orange

Below are some of her favorite breakfasts:

Smoothie	Granola with coconut yogurt
Waffles or pancakes	Eggs and avocado

Bonus Kids' Snacks

Surprise Blueberry Mango Fruit Roll Up
Page 137

Yogurt Berry Fruit Roll Up
Page 138

Slow Cooker Applesauce Cups
Page 139

Berry Kombucha Jello
Page 141

Surprise Blueberry Mango Roll Up

Prep Time: 10 minutes
Wait Time: 4 hours

Grain free, added sugar free, gluten free, dairy free *Serves: 6–8*

Directions

1. Blend all ingredients.
2. Place on a dehydrator mat with no holes.
3. Dehydrate at 135ºF for 3–5 hours. If you don't have a dehydrator, pour mixture on a piece of parchment paper on a cookie sheet and bake at 170ºF for 3–5 hours or until dry.

Ingredients

1 cup blueberries
1 cup chopped mango
Handful of spinach

Yogurt Berry Fruit Roll Up

Prep Time: 10 minutes
Wait Time: 4 hours

Grain free, gluten free, dairy free   *Serves: 6–8*

Directions

1. Blend all ingredients.
2. Place on a dehydrator mat with no holes and dehydrate at 135ºF for 3–5 hours. If you don't have a dehydrator, pour the mixture on a piece of parchment paper on a cookie sheet and bake at 170°F for 3–5 hours or until dry.

Ingredients

2 cups organic yogurt or coconut yogurt

1 cup mixed berries

1 teaspoon vanilla

1–2 tablespoon honey

Slow Cooker Applesauce Cups

Prep Time: 15 minutes
Wait Time: 4 hours

Grain free, sugar free, gluten free, dairy free   *Serves: 8–10*

Making these and freezing some in either those freezable pouches or in ice trays are perfect snacks for a busy toddler. My daughter finds it satisfying to squeeze applesauce out of pouches, so this is usually my method. Don't be afraid to experiment with other flavors; you might add some berries or use pears instead of apples.

Directions

1. Peel and core apples and cut into cubes.
2. Add all ingredients to a slow cooker and stir.
3. Let cook for 3–4 hours. Apples should be very soft and tender. If apples are sticking to the bottom, just add a bit more water.
4. Once the apples are tender, purée or mash them.

Ingredients

3 pounds apples
1 teaspoon cinnamon
1 1/2 cups water
1 tablespoon lemon juice
1/8 teaspoon sea salt

Berry Kombucha Jello

Prep Time: 15 minutes
Wait Time: 3–4 hours

Grain free, sugar free, gluten free, dairy free   *Serves: 8–10*

Directions

1. Place kombucha in a bowl and sprinkle the gelatin over it. Set aside.
2. Heat the juice in a saucepan until it is almost boiling.
3. Thoroughly mix the juice and kombucha together.
4. Pour into a 9" × 13" pan or jello molds and place in the refrigerator for 4 or more hours.

Ingredients

2 cups 100% pure fruit juice
2 cups homemade kombucha
3 tablespoons grass-fed gelatin

If you don't have kombucha, you can substitute more juice. If you have an excess of kombucha, you can just use kombucha, but you should heat it less. If it is all kombucha, the jello is a bit runnier, so you'll need to add a little more gelatin to it.

Fermented Foods

Fermented foods have gained great popularity in recent years, primarily due to increased awareness of the microbiome and the harmful effects of antibiotics on the good bacteria in the digestive system.

Fermented foods are a staple in our household, and I make all my own fermentations to save on costs! Some of the more popular fermented foods are sauerkraut, kombucha, kefir, yogurt, and kimchi. In my kitchen, the most common ones are kefir, yogurt, and kombucha. Grapes get fermented into wine, cabbage gets fermented into sauerkraut, green tea gets fermented into kombucha, milk gets fermented to yogurt or kefir, etc. The idea of fermenting a food for themselves seems foreign to some people, but it is actually a fairly common practice.

Fermented Bonus Recipes

Kefir
Page 145

Kombucha
Page 147

Kefir

Prep Time: 10 minutes
Wait Time: 24 hours

Grain free, sugar free, gluten free   *Serves: 4–6*

*Kefir should not smell or taste rotten. If it does, strain the grains, clean them with filtered water, and start over.

Directions

1. Sterilize 2 quart-sized jars.
2. Place the kefir grains in one jar and fill the jar with milk.
3. Place the cloth and secure on top of jar with a rubber band.
4. Keep the jar on the countertop out of sunlight for one day. You can shake it every so often.
5. After 24 hours, strain the grains through a strainer into a mixing bowl.
6. Transfer the liquid to the clean jar and smell and taste it. If it is thick, tangy, and a little fizzy, it's perfect!
7. Keep the kefir in the refrigerator.
8. Move the kefir grains from the strainer into the first jar.
9. Repeat the process to make another batch.
10. If you want to save the grains for a later batch, cover them with milk and place them in the refrigerator.

Ingredients

4 tablespoons kefir grains
1 quart grass-fed milk
2 Coffee filters or cloth that is breathable
non-metal mixing bowl
wooden spoon
non-metal strainer

Kombucha

Prep Time: 30 minutes
Wait Time: 7–10 days

Grain free, gluten free, dairy free   *Serves: 4–6*

Directions

1. To start, boil 12 cups of water.
2. Just before boiling, stir in the sugar and tea bags.
3. Take the pot off the heat and set aside to cool.
4. Once tea has completely cooled, take out the tea bags.
5. Pour the cooled tea into your gallon jar.
6. Place the SCOBY on top in the jar and pour the starter liquid on top.
7. Cover with breathable cloth and seal with a rubber band. Place in a cupboard (or another warm, dark place) for 7–10 days.
8. Taste the kombucha after 7 or 8 days to see if it is ready. Less fermenting time will result in a sweeter taste, and more time gives it a more vinegar-like taste.
9. When the kombucha is ready, place 2 cups of liquid in a bowl and set it aside (this will serve as the starter liquid for your next batch).
10. Now you can either pour the kombucha into smaller jars and place it in the refrigerator, or you can do a second fermentation to flavor your kombucha.*

*To make flavored kombucha, place fruit in the smaller jars (about 10% of the jar) and then pour the kombucha over the fruit. Put the smaller jars back in the cupboard for 2–3 days, and then in the refrigerator.

Ingredients

1 mother SCOBY (Symbiotic Culture of Bacteria and Yeast)
2 cups starter kombucha
12 cups boiling water
5–8 organic green tea bags
1 cup sugar*
Jars with plastic lids
1 gallon-sized "pickle" jar
Rubber band
Thin dish cloth or coffee filter (untreated)

Dr. Tom Stetson

Contributing author Dr. Tom Stetson has dedicated his life to helping families reach their optimal health potential. Since graduating from Palmer College of Chiropractic, he has become a sought-after speaker and has consulted with thousands of patients regarding their nutrition needs and more. Dr. Stetson's multi-faceted approach includes cutting-edge metabolic nutritional testing and allergy testing.